MY SKY

The Flights & Times of Bill Cox

By Bill Cox

JP Media LLC
Publisher of Cessna Owner Organization and Piper Owner Society
www.cessnaowner.org
www.piperowner.org

Publisher & President
Diana Jones

Vice President & Editor
Rocky Landsverk

Editor
Katie Holliday-Greenley

Senior Graphic Designer
Bill Kuffel

First Edition
Printed in the United States of America

Cessna Owner Organization
Piper Owner Society
N7528 Aanstad Rd.
P.O. Box 5000
Iola, WI 54945-5000
jpmediallc.com
cessnaowner.org
piperowner.org

MY SKY
The Flights & Times of Bill Cox

Acknowledgments

This book would not have been possible without the constant encouragement of so many friends and readers of my monthly columns and stories in a few dozen publications over the last 40 years.

If articles are relatively short, books can be truly gargantuan undertakings. One thing I've learned from my friend Rod Machado (who has a half-dozen of his own very successful books in print) is that a book may be only 40-50 times the length of a magazine article, but plan on expending at least 200 times the effort.

This project has been in the works for about 10 years. Some of it appeared – in slightly different forms – in my monthly column "Cross Country Log," as feature articles in *Plane & Pilot Magazine*, in *Pilot Journal*, as "Lessons From the Logbook" in *PIPERS* magazine and *Cessna Owner* magazine, in *Flying* magazine, or in *AOPA Pilot*. Some chapters are original and unpublished.

From that long list, JP Media LLC — publishers of *PIPERS* and *Cessna Owner* — get credit for asking me, "Hey would you like to publish a book?" So, we did.

Much of the subject matter has to do with 40 years of international delivery flying to Africa, Australia, Japan, Europe, the Middle East, or anywhere else someone was foolish enough to send me.

This book is dedicated to my wife and soulmate,
Dr. Peggy Herrera, a fellow pilot without
whose encouragement, it would never have
been completed or published.

Photo by Jack Fleetwood (*www.jackfleetwood.com*)

Send in the Clouds

Pilots see clouds in a different way, and they are grateful.

You must travel to feel one with clouds. Through the miracle of several thousand cooperative turbine and piston engines (and a few dozen cranky ones) over 50 something years, I've witnessed clouds in most of their forms.

In my part of the sky, at least the part I watch most often, Southern California, we don't see many clouds. In late spring through early fall, fog creeps slowly in from the ocean, covering Southern California with a 1,000-foot blanket of soft-white, semi-diaphanous fluff. For most of the rest of the year, the Los Angeles Basin manifests more clement atmospherics, the dry, desert climate of Palm Springs (but without the heat) rather than the wet, cold rain of San Francisco.

You must travel to feel one with clouds. Through the miracle of several thousand cooperative turbine and piston engines (and a few dozen cranky ones) over 50 something years, I've witnessed clouds in most of their forms. I've watched thunderstorms in Kansas, Australia, and South Africa, monsters of rage and madness, campaigning across Wichita, the Outback, or the Serengeti, leaving mayhem in their wake. I've been terrified by typhoons in Guam, Singapore, and the Philippines – insane, swirling masses of black-on-white, churning the ocean into monster waves.

I've endured blizzards in Canada and Greenland, white-outs that relegated instrument approaches to near-impossibilities. I've caromed through marshmallow cumulus in the South Pacific, swum in monsoonal rainclouds over Indonesia, and climbed through orange sandstorms above the arid Sahara and the waterless Kalahari.

None of that makes me an expert on clouds, but it has certainly introduced me to my fair share of sky, from angry to insidiously calm. I've become something of a student of clouds, if a relatively uninformed one, always curious as to the how and why of the sky.

I can't help but envy the astronauts their high station, looking down on the Earth from an elliptical orbit 200 miles up. They have a totally unobstructed view of clouds over much of the globe, and with the advantage of 16 orbits a day, they gain a new perspective of weather systems every 90 minutes.

High cirrus clouds must have special meaning for me, as I had a white German shepherd named after them (now long gone to the great doghouse in the sky). Flying to Chile or Argentina, most pilots aviate down the west coast of South America, keeping the Andes on the left, and I've watched silky filaments of mare's tail cirrus lingering above the spine of the Andes along much of that route.

Navigating through the Pan American pass east of Santiago en route to Buenos Aires, I've witnessed giant, lens-shaped lenticulars, motionless at 35,000 feet, hovering above Cerro Aconcagua, tallest mountain in South America. Lennies, as hardly anyone calls them, are congenial companions, stationary symbols of the collective power of mountains and sky.

Unfortunately, all clouds aren't so benign. Some are filled with ice, others can house monstrous electrical storms, and a few can be home to whirling death. A dozen years ago, on a trip from Los Angeles to Singapore in an A36TC Bonanza, I was flying the last leg from Darwin across Bali and up the Indonesian chain. Sporadic thunderstorms are practically an everyday occurrence in that part of the world, and they were waiting for me with muscular bodies and cauliflower tops as I tracked northwest, starting at 12,000 feet and gradually being forced lower, trying to stay beneath the worst of them. The cumulonimbus clouds wrapped around me all the way to the minimum en route altitude, and I could see occasional flashes of gold inside the clouds, lighting the cockpit with a strange, iridescent, yellow glow.

The Stormscope pointed out the worst concentrations of static discharge, and with nothing better to do than continue, I dodged around them as best I could. I flew on toward Singapore and finally, 13 hours after leaving Darwin, landed at Seletar Airport (WSSL) in the same murky, semi-darkness, punctuated by now-remote lightning partially obscured by the mist. I cleaned up the seat and vowed never to do that again.

Once, a few years back, flying the first Extra 400 to be ferried across the Atlantic, I was out of Iqaluit, Nunavut, Canada, headed for Wabush, Labrador. It was midsummer on the Arctic Circle, so the sun had been up all night, and I was up early, too, hoping to clear customs in Bangor, Maine, and make it to Indianapolis for the overnight, then on to my destination of Phoenix the following day.

Just south of Ungava Bay, I spotted the first of what became dozens of the strangest clouds I'd ever seen. They looked like a cross between the Pillsbury Doughboy and the Michelin Man. These were strange, plump, white doughnuts, well-defined and stacked five to six layers tall, perhaps 400 feet from top to bottom, fatter in the middle than on the top and bottom. They drifted aimlessly at 8,000 feet along the coast of the Labrador Sea.

Naturally, I'd left my camera at home, so the best I could do later when I talked to my favorite weatherman in California, Jeff Kopps, was forward a sketch. No one had any idea what they were.

Most clouds aren't that complex. Meteorologists such as Jeff can explain exactly how they form, mature, and die. Water becomes cloud becomes ice becomes water.

If the science is almost silly simple, the imagery is pure imagination. To those of us who study them and feel privileged to travel among them, clouds are more than simple meteorological phenomena. Look ... there's one that looks like a three-masted schooner over there. That's the Empire State Building out front. And anyone can tell, that's obviously a lion's head off to the right, complete with mane.

Clouds can often be guideposts, especially when several airplanes are trying to join up over the ocean. Sure, we could use GPS, but it's often more fun to say, "Hey, Jon, let's meet at 10,000 feet by the big cumulus that looks like mouse ears."

Clouds can often be guideposts, especially when several airplanes are trying to join up over the ocean. Sure, we could use GPS, but it's often more fun to say, "Hey, Jon, let's meet at 10,000 feet by the big cumulus that looks like mouse ears."

If we occasionally treat clouds in jest, they can sometimes exact revenge. While ferrying a '58 Baron from the West Coast to Cleveland following a double engine change, I was flying late in the afternoon through walls of cumulus over Indiana, punching through a cloud, emerging into the clear for a few seconds, then repeating the process.

Suddenly, I broke out of a cumulus and instantly knew I was dead. Another airplane had just emerged from the wall of white straight ahead and was coming directly at me, obviously flying at the wrong altitude. I had only the briefest millisecond to brace for the impact.

In an instant, I collided with my own black shadow, projected on the cloud ahead by the sun behind.

I could almost hear the clouds chuckling.

2

Mt. McKinley

There's Something About Mountains

Far from menacing monsters, mountains can be your best friends.

The Pan-American Highway threads its way steeply uphill out of Santiago, Chile, climbing into the rarified air of South America toward the high Andes. The road rises with the terrain, slowly ascending through switchbacks and turnabouts until someone noticed that a conventional highway was becoming impractical, so they decided to build a tunnel.

Unfortunately, airplanes can't use tunnels. As I look straight east at the solid rock ridge that seems taller than I could possibly fly in a poor, defenseless, normally aspirated Cessna 207, I marvel at the sheer poetry of the mountains.

In fact, poetry prevails in the Andes, from Caracas at the top of the continent to Tierra del Fuego at the bottom. Here in the middle, I can see the high foothills of Cerro Aconcagua as it reaches for the flight levels. Struggling through 11,000 feet, I'm not even half as tall. Aconcagua is the highest peak in the Western Hemisphere, piercing the clouds to an elevation of nearly 23,000 feet. And I thought McKinley was big.

There's little relief on the south side of the pass. Cerro Tupungato, the Andes' second highest mountain at 21,500 feet, guards the southern approach, jealous of my artificial altitude and determined to be bigger than I am. It wins.

Somewhere to the south of Tupungato back in 1972, a twin turboprop carrying an Uruguayan rugby team crashed in the high mountains, and 16 survivors overcame incredible odds to live 72 days under extreme conditions before being rescued.

This is the portal through the High Andes between Santiago, Chile, and Buenos Aires, Argentina, an unforgiving V of granite, grudgingly allowing only some of those who dare try to pass unmolested. There is no malevolent or mysterious accident triangle here, no devils or dragons reside, but it is a region of thin air and sometimes violent weather, often terribly unforgiving of any mistake.

The mountains taper down to a series of high hills 300 miles south, but no, I have to do it the hard way. I struggle to surmount the lowest point of the ridge, wave soaring with condors for more altitude. The walls of the pass, I'm told, feature occasional reflections from aluminum airplane parts, once attached to living, breathing Cessnas, Pipers, Fairchilds, and de Havillands — memorials to others who weren't so fortunate as I hope to be.

And yet, despite the high rocks' disapproving, ominous frowns, looking down on me from 4-mile heights, there is a kind of beauty to these semi-vertical edifices. I suppose my real appreciation stems from having been raised in Alaska and New Mexico where mountains dominate practically every horizon, and to have subsequently lived around them most of my life.

I spent my teenage years in Anchorage, and I used to look north on those bitingly cold, incredibly clear winter days and see the dramatic white dome of McKinley peeking over the horizon, shining in the sun from 150 miles away. Unlike the jagged blades of rock that top Everest and Annapurna, McKinley always seemed benign and friendly, a happy, rounded marshmallow of a mountain. I used to think, "Perhaps I'll take a stroll up the side of it some afternoon," not knowing that Denali (the Native American name for it) is infamous in the climbing community for some of the worst weather conditions of any mountain.

Later, 2,500 miles south in Albuquerque, I lived hard by the peaks of Sandia, and still later in Southern California, I flew the length of the Owens Valley, staring up at Mt. Whitney, marveling at the majesty of the jagged Sierra Nevada. There were times when the rising terrain fostered wild up and down drafts, and my love for tall rocks was tempered by gritted teeth and seat belts pulled as tight as I could get them.

Still, there was always the wonderful, Sheepherder bread of Schat's Bakery in Bishop to look forward to. I used to fly my first airplane, a Globe Swift, 200 miles to Bishop just for the great bread, the $100 loaf of bread rather than a cheeseburger. It seemed worth it at the time. I hope Schat's is still there [Editor's Note: It is].

Some pilots regard mountains as the enemy. I've always considered them friends. Learn to read them, envision the wind flowing across them like water cascading over rocks in a stream, fly the appropriate slope, and you may be able to appreciate free climb or tailwinds. High terrain can also serve as a buffer to help hold bad weather at higher elevation and provide room to fly underneath.

When the weather is good, mountains can serve as navigation beacons for hundreds of miles. McKinley stands like a sentinel practically in the middle of Alaska. When visibility is good, you can see the perpetually white mushroom peak from 200 miles away in all directions.

Some pilots regard mountains as the enemy. I've always considered them friends. Learn to read them, envision the wind flowing across them like water cascading over rocks in a stream, fly the appropriate slope, and you may be able to appreciate free climb or tailwinds.

Once, 25 years ago during a bright September morning, I was flying a Cheyenne III from Anchorage to Point Barrow. Looking down in air as clear as Chablis and as smooth as sable. Denali was looking back, benign, and spectacular, with no telltale plume of snow blowing off the top, suggesting light winds at the peak.

I couldn't resist the temptation, so I asked Anchorage center if I could drop down and skim across the muscular, snow-capped peak. What I thought was an original idea was apparently old hat to the controller, as he immediately approved my deviation in the most bored voice possible.

The air was dead calm as I leveled at 20,500 feet, 200 feet above the summit. It wasn't Everest, and I didn't imagine I was Col. Robert Scott of the Flying Tigers, buzzing the world's tallest mountain in 1942, but it was still a thrill. (For details, read Scott's book, *God Is My Copilot*.)

In the Southwest U.S., Navajo Mountain, a huge, bulbous hillock of rock east of Page, Arizona, also serves as a waypoint for pilots. It's only about 10,300 feet tall, but it stands all alone at the north end of the Painted Desert, 5,000 feet above local terrain. You can spot it from any direction for 100 miles.

Traveling along the West Coast in clear conditions, you can fly north with a series of huge mountains as guideposts. In Northern California, there's Mt. Shasta; then, the Three Sisters and Mt. Hood in Oregon; Mt. St. Helens and Mt. Rainier in Washington pointing the way to Seattle, and finally Mt. Baker on the Canadian border near Vancouver. I've only seen the full panoply of volcanos two or three times in 40 years of flying, but it's nothing short of splendiferous.

9

Pampas landscapes in Cordillera de Los Andes, Peru, South America

On this day in December, my passage across the Andes is anticlimactic, if that's even possible amid such a magnificent display of topography. I clear the pass into Argentina without incident, following the advice of my friends the Condors. They soar effortlessly above me and watch my loud, comparatively ugly, awkward metal beast struggling to match their grace.

Overloaded and almost tapped out of climb, my Cessna finally skims a few hundred feet above the lonely, metal, Chilean research

station built directly on the nadir of the pass, and I fly out into the huge valley above Mendoza, Argentina, with the Patagonian Desert to my right. How could anyone not love mountains?

These days, the mountains' value as navigation waypoints has been diminished. Pilotage has become a lost art, and dead reckoning is now automatic with a $500 GPS. The satellites have relegated the art of navigation to a few keystrokes, but mountains can still highlight a route and provide comfort to help you recognize the hills of home.

For the Birds

**Birds are aerodynamic marvels the likes
of which man can never hope to emulate.**

I've been an accidental student of bird flight for as long as I've been alive — and that's a long time. Growing up in Alaska provided me with a huge selection of birds, from ducks and geese to swans, sea gulls, and snoodled gannets. They'd migrate north and south during spring and fall, respectively, landing in the local lakes and rivers of south-central Alaska to rest and refuel for the long flights ahead.

Perhaps best of all, I used to ride my bike down to Lake Hood, the world's largest seaplane base then and now, to watch birds and floatplanes transition from water to sky and back again. I'd monitor the flocks of ducks and geese in impromptu short-field competition with Cessna 180s, Super Cubs, Maules, and Beavers; all, fortunately, on floats.

The manmade machines never stood a chance. One look at the competitors explained why. In contrast to the graceful wings and swept body of a mallard, even the most modern seaplane looked clumsy and crude, like something a Klingon might fly into battle.

I studied and photographed birds while in high school (at the risk of being considered a dweeb), read what I could about how birds fly, and compared that with man's primitive efforts to lift himself into the sky.

Living in Alaska made ornithology an easy, if unlikely, hobby for a teenage boy whose dominant interests included (first things first, though not necessarily in this order) girls, target shooting, girls, cars, and, of course, girls. Funniest thing, I never mentioned to my friends that I was into bird watching for fear of being branded a nerd. If I had, they probably would have assumed I was using the British term for girls.

I learned that birds are aerodynamic marvels the likes of which mere man can never hope to emulate or understand. Though there are no rotary-wing birds, many of the existing varieties can lift off with virtually zero takeoff roll, then land (water?) in the same distance. With the benefit of wings that can articulate almost infinitely through sweep, dihedral, and angle of attack, birds can perform maneuvers that would leave even Patty Wagstaff or Sean Tucker green with envy.

I lived in Venice, Florida, for a year back in the late '60s and used to walk down to the beach to watch sea gulls fight for the breadcrumbs I'd take with me. I was always amazed at how quickly a totally empty beach, with nary a bird in sight, could turn into an instant aviary after I threw the first handful of crumbs into the air.

A dozen gulls would seemingly materialize from nowhere. By the second handful, there would be 30-40 sea gulls crowding the airspace, squawking, and snapping up bread in mid-air, performing aerobatics that made a lomcevak look tame by comparison. With a combination of wing warping, variable sweep, asymmetric lift, fully controllable dihedral, and a variety of other tricks, those sea gulls showed me maneuvers I could never duplicate in an Extra or Pitts.

I've watched hummingbirds perform seemingly impossible turns, darting left or right with apparent immunity to the *g*-forces involved, and I've even witnessed them flying backwards. In fact, hummingbirds feature a resilient bone structure that provides both strength and flexibility to allow amazing proficiency at hovering and changing direction in an instant. A NASA researcher using a high-speed camera calculated their turns and twists at a maximum of 10*g*. That's more than the most aggressive fighter pilot can endure and well outside the limits of America's best jet fighters.

Birds have proven their superiority to humans (at least, this human) and airplanes on numerous other occasions. In Chapter 2 I mentioned that while trying to coax a Cessna 207 across the Pan-American Pass in the Chilean Andes of South America east of Santiago, I spotted a huge condor soaring on thermals near the ridge, his wings seemingly immobile as he somehow magically arced uphill. His wingspan must have been nearly 10 feet.

I took the hint and joined him on the opposite side of the thermal. I followed the condor in his ascent for several thousand feet, watching him monitor my curious aluminum bird, mimicking his every action. I worked the lift until I had what I hoped was enough altitude to cross the ridge, then broke away and managed to sneak across the high rocks to Argentina before the big Cessna could descend into the granite.

It may be a local myth, but the story was going around several years ago that a Lan Chile crew operating a Boeing 737 at FL330, spotted an Andean Condor cruising high above 23,000-foot Cerro Aconcagua, the Andes' highest mountain.

Another time in the '80s, I was flying my Mooney above Northern California, cruising at perhaps 150 knots, when what looked like a bird overtook me on the left and passed by at least 25-30 knots faster. My best speculation was that it was a peregrine falcon. They're allegedly capable of speeds in excess of 180 knots, and this one seemed to be doing that or more.

A bird also may have helped me find my destination in the middle of the Pacific Ocean. In the late '80s, long before the advent of GPS, I was flying an Australia-bound Navajo below an overcast of thunderstorms and miscellaneous meteorological misery when the nondirectional beacon at Majuro went off the air when I was 340 nm from my destination. Majuro is about 2,000 nm from Honolulu, and except for Johnston Island, 700 miles out, there's not even a rock sticking up to navigate by. I had little choice but to find the atoll by dead reckoning, desperately hoping the navigation method wouldn't wind up being too descriptive.

Fortunately, I spotted a flock of sea gulls below holding a steady course, their wings barely fluttering in the updrafts off the water. They seemed to be flying in the same general direction I was, so I turned slightly left to follow their heading and spotted the ring atoll two hours later. It turned out there'd been a power failure on the island, and someone had allowed the gas tank for the NDB's automatic backup generator to run dry. Fortunately, the sea gulls didn't need the NDB.

I've been fortunate to fly a wide variety of airplanes in the last half-century, some that could perform some amazing tricks. None of them, however, was 10 percent as talented as even the simplest bird.

Birds have an impressive ability to maintain flight for long periods of time, partially a function of their capacity for reading the wind. This, in turn, leads to an innate facility at dynamic soaring, the capacity to convert horizontal winds to vertical lift. This is especially useful over the ocean where a rolling sea imparts nearly continuous, minor updrafts.

My buddy bush pilot Butch Patterson and I once set down on a remote Oregon lake in his float-equipped Skyhawk and watched several bald eagles glide effortlessly for what seemed like hours, occasionally swooping down to snap up a fish in the lake or a mouse on the shore and deliver it to their nests.

One small, migratory flyer — a bar-tailed godwit — may hold the record for sustained flight without refueling. The bird was tagged and fitted with a GPS encoder in Anchorage, then tracked by satellite from Alaska to New Zealand nonstop in nine days. That's nearly 8,100 nm without changing tanks.

I've been fortunate to fly a wide variety of airplanes in the last half-century, some that could perform some amazing tricks. None of them, however, was 10% as talented as even the simplest bird.

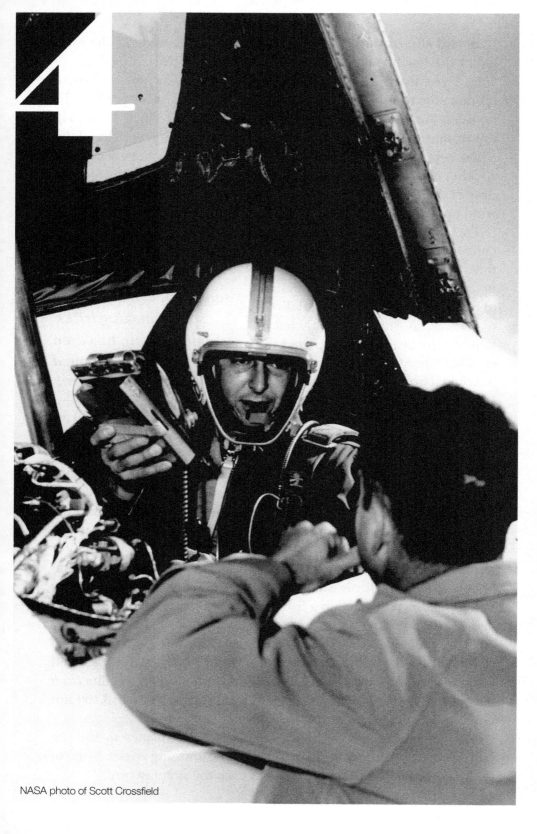

4

NASA photo of Scott Crossfield

Scotty

Scott Crossfield was a hero, especially to those who knew him.

Like most folks who were privileged to know him, I regarded Scotty as an aeronautical genius, on the same level as Roy Lopresti.

I was sitting in the Victor Aviation booth at the SUN 'n FUN International Fly-In & Expo in 1992 discussing engine overhauls with an Aerostar owner when, out of the corner of my eye, I saw a "more info" card drop into the glass container. I could clearly read the name "Crossfield" on it.

That could only be one person, I thought. I excused myself and hurried down the aisle after the older gentlemen who'd dropped the card into the jug. Yes, it was Scott Crossfield, the famous rocket test pilot from the '50s and '60s, and he was interested in a new Victor Black Edition engine for his 1960 Cessna 210.

Scotty was gracious enough to stop and talk with me for a few minutes and even agreed to a taped interview for a story. He came back to the booth where we sat down and discussed engines, airplanes in general, and some of his experiences in the world of Mach 2 and Mach 3 aircraft.

Over the next dozen years, I was proud to count Scotty as a friend. He did wind up with a Victor engine in his Cessna and was so impressed that he became a spokesman for the company. We'd only see each other a half-dozen times a year — SUN 'n FUN, EAA AirVenture Oshkosh, the Reno Air Races, the AOPA convention, or the Albuquerque Balloon Fiesta — but every time we got together, I learned something new about flying.

Like most folks who were privileged to know him, I regarded Scotty as an aeronautical genius on the same level as Roy Lopresti. He was a Navy fighter pilot during World War II who went on to work in aerodynamics, aircraft design, and test flying. Most people know Scott as the test pilot on the first 30 flights of the X-15, the first man to fly Mach 2 (in the Douglas D-558 II Skyrocket), and the first to survive flying Mach 3. Not many are aware he was also one of the X-15's primary designers.

When Scott left Edwards Air Force Base as chief NACA test pilot in 1955 to join the North American X-15 design team, he had

99 flights in rocket-powered aircraft, making him by far the world's most experienced rocket pilot.

Sadly, we lost Scotty in April 2006. Perhaps appropriately, it was in an airplane. He was flying his beloved Cessna 210 beneath convective weather in Georgia on his way home to Virginia, and for reasons undetermined, the Cessna disintegrated. Investigators at the scene reported the debris field was consistent with an in-flight breakup and scattered over a distance of 1 mile.

I was as stunned as everyone at the news, but my memories of Scott Crossfield are more happy than sad. At age 84, he'd had a good run, and he was grateful for having been in the right place at the right time to fly the X-planes. When I saw him a week before he died, he was still happy and upbeat, with a perpetual twinkle in his eye, a smile on his face and a joke in his heart.

As you might expect of an aeronautical engineer steeped with six decades of experience, Scotty kept his airplane in near-perfect mechanical condition, but he never cared much about appearances. The Cessna was painted a hideous green, yellow, and white — it may have been the original paint job. Everything worked and the airplane ran well, but I never would have guessed it belonged to Scott Crossfield.

Back in 1994, when I was flying new engine installations for Victor Aviation, I flew with Scotty in his 210 following the Black Edition overhaul. He was gracious to offer me the left seat and said he wanted to see how Victor recommended he operate his 260-hp Continental engine.

When I explained that Victor suggested flying it hard for at least the first 50 hours, Scotty quietly commented that he liked to run the engine at no more than 55%. It seemed somehow incongruous that the man who surpassed even Chuck Yeager in the quest for speed was so conservative with his own airplane.

In view of that seeming contradiction, it should come as no great surprise that Scott was an enthusiastic fan of the Wright brothers. He felt the Wrights paved the way for those who came later. It may be true that two wrongs don't make a right, but two Wrights made an aeroplane.

In a 1988 interview in *Aviation Week & Space Technology*, Crossfield said, "My role models were the Wright brothers. They created the whole circle. They got involved in the concept, the criteria, the requirements, the details, the manufacturing and quality control, and the managing of a new and innovative work. In 1898, they established a program to fly in 1903. They stuck to that plan except when they had to deviate and build their own engine. They built wind tunnels, and they did fly in 1903. Actually, they were the first systems integration engineers, and they gave us the example as the way to do business today."

Perhaps partially because of his reverence for the Wrights, Scott was chosen to lead the team intended to fly the 100th anniversary Wright Flyer replica in 2003. Bad weather and a lack of wind at Kittyhawk on December 17 doomed that effort to failure, but Scott's team gave it a good try.

With more than a half-century in the industry, Scotty accrued more aviation accolades and awards than anyone else I can think of, far too many to list here. While he was well aware of his own abilities, he often manifested a self-deprecating sense of humor about his experiences.

In his book, *Always Another Dawn*, he wrote about dead-sticking the X-15 and a variety of other low lift-to-drag test planes back into Edwards, some with glide ratios as poor as 3-to-1. (A typical general aviation single has a glide ratio of about 10-to-1.) One of those was an F-100 Super Sabre that experienced an engine fire during a test flight. Scott shut down the engine to put out the fire but elected to stay with the airplane rather than follow the military manual advice to point the nose in a safe direction and punch out. Crossfield dead-sticked the airplane back to Edwards ("It was one of the best landings I'd ever made"), then "proceeded to violate a cardinal rule of aviation; never try tricks

> *Scott Crossfield on the Wright Brothers:*
> *"Actually, they were the first systems integration engineers, and they gave us the example as the way to do business today."*

with a compromised airplane," he reported. "I (decided I'd) end my flight with a flourish, a spectacular wind-up. I would snake the stricken F-100 up the ramp and bring it to (a) stop right in front of the NACA hangar.

"According to the F-100 handbook, the hydraulic brake system was good for three 'cycles,' engine out … three pumps on the brakes, and that proved exactly right," Scotty continued. "The F-100 was moving at about 15 mph when I turned up the ramp. I hit the brakes once, twice, three times. The plane slowed but not quite enough. I hit the brakes a fourth time — and my foot went clear to the floorboards. My plane bored steadily on toward the side wall of the hangar. The nose of the F-100 crunched through the corrugated aluminum, punching out an 8-inch steel I-beam.

"Chuck Yeager never let me forget that incident. He drew many laughs at congregations of pilots by opening his talks (with): 'Well, the sonic wall was mine. The hangar wall was Crossfield's.' That's the way it was at Edwards, hero one minute, bum the next."

Those of us who knew him never regarded Scott Crossfield as anything but a hero.

5

Glacier Girl is second from the left in this Heritage
Flight at EAA AirVenture Oshkosh in 2010. Flying
here (from left) are an F-4 Phantom, *Glacier Girl*, an
F-15, and P-38 *Ruff Stuff*. Photo courtesy of EAA

The Odyssey of Glacier Girl

Famed airplane comes home.

1942 — A flight of six P-38s and two B-17s departs Sondre Stromfjord, Greenland, for Reykjavik, Iceland, on their way to the World War II European Theater of Operations as part of Operation Bolero. It's an ambitious project, initiated by Gen. Hap Arnold, tired of seeing his aircraft ride cargo ships to the bottom of the Atlantic, victims of Hitler's dreaded U-boats.

Halfway to Reykjavik, the flight encounters thick clouds and icing conditions and turns back for Greenland, only to discover the weather has worsened at Sondre Stromfjord as well. Low on fuel and with no place left to go, all eight airplanes crash land on the Greenland Ice Cap, and all 27 members of the eight crews escape uninjured. Nine days later, the group is rescued and evacuated to the east coast of Greenland. The airplanes remain on the cap where they came to rest. They are slowly swallowed by the snow and ice, gradually becoming a part of the world's largest ice island.

Fast forward 50 years. Warbird expert Bob Cardin leads a team of adventurers out onto the ice to recover one of the aircraft. The 10th expedition to make the effort, Cardin's group battles blizzard conditions and minus 29 degrees Celsius temperatures, and finally succeeds in retrieving a partially crushed P-38 from 266 feet below the surface of the Greenland Ice Cap. The team transports the disassembled airplane by ski-equipped DC-3 to the port of Kulusuk and ships it to Savannah, Georgia.

Ten years and $4 million of restoration expense later, owner Ed Shoffer watches his P-38, now affectionately known by its new name, Glacier Girl, fly again for the first time since 1942. Planes of Fame Museum owner Steve Hinton, one of the world's most knowledgeable warbird pilots, campaigns the Lockheed on the air show circuit all over the U.S. for five years. Now, it's summer 2007 and time to complete the flight to England as part of Operation Bolero II.

Picture this: I'm facing backwards in Rod Lewis' Pilatus PC-12 200 nm out over the Labrador Sea. Snuggled into echelon formation 10 feet off the Pilatus' left wing, Steve Hinton guides perhaps the world's most famous warbird, the P-38 *Glacier Girl*. Ten feet off the right wing, Mustang expert Ed Shipley flies *Miss Velma*, a newly rebuilt TF-51 Mustang. It's a warbird fan's dream.

On the face of it, the mission might not seem that difficult. *Glacier Girl* needed to fly from Chino, California, to Duxford, England, for an appearance at several early-July air shows. I was hired to help expedite the Atlantic crossing, deal with ATC in four countries, provide some educated guesses on weather and routes, and recommend hotels and restaurants for the crew of *Glacier Girl* and *Miss Velma* as well as the Pilatus and a Citation Sovereign jet support aircraft.

The P-38's new owner, Rod Lewis of Lewis Energy in San Antonio, Texas, has graciously provided ample assets for the trip. In addition to Hinton and Shipley, we have a total support group of 11, including Hinton, Loftis, Cardin, Lewis, mechanics, photographers, wives, and me, the least valuable member of the team.

Glacier Girl before the renovation. Photo courtesy of EAA.

The plan was for the PC-12 to shepherd the two fighters across the pond in loose formation while the Sovereign charged ahead to make certain all was ready for the warbirds. Range wasn't a particular problem. With drop tanks in place, both the Lightning and Mustang could manage an easy 1,100 nm, and the longest leg would be only about 680 nm.

Weather permitting, our trip would attempt to retrace the planned original Operation Bolero route: Presque Isle, Maine; Goose Bay, Labrador, Canada; Frobisher Bay (now Iqaluit), Nunavut, Canada; Sondre Stromfjord, Greenland; Reykjavik, Iceland; and on to England.

It was the "weather permitting" part that worried me. WWII fighters were never designed for operation in icing conditions or hard IFR, so Hinton and Shipley needed to make the trip in pure VFR conditions if at all possible. In my 150 flights across the Atlantic over the last 30 years, I can count the number of pure VFR crossings I've made on the thumbs of one hand.

The trip started in Teterboro, New Jersey, with a media frenzy more befitting Kim Kardashian than a 65-year-old warbird. Hinton, Shipley, Rod Lewis, and team leader Bob Cardin gave dozens of interviews, and *Glacier Girl* and *Miss Velma* flew by the Statue of Liberty for the cameras before we finally launched for Presque Isle, Maine, a day later.

Our reception at Presque Isle was smaller but equally enthusiastic. We were delayed for two days in Presque Isle for weather, then dispatched Lewis' Sovereign jet ahead to Goose Bay beneath the weather at 5,500 feet to scout the route. (Sovereign pilot D.P. Loftis commented, "We certainly didn't set any speed record, but we may have for fuel burn.") When the Sovereign pilots called on the satellite phone and advised the route was relatively clear and ice-free, we launched with the PC-12 and the two fighters for Goose.

There was another two-day delay in Goose Bay for parts for the Mustang, and bad weather in Northern Labrador and Nunavut made the original Bolero route inadvisable, so we were relegated to the southern route.

Now, we're finally on our way across the Atlantic on the first overwater leg — Goose Bay to Narsarsuaq. The atmospherics are near-perfect, with clear skies, nearly 24 hours of daylight in late June and even slight tailwinds.

We depart Goose Bay at 0900 local and begin tracking out over the water toward Greenland. The icebergs begin to appear 100 miles offshore, right on schedule, and this has all the makings of a near-perfect crossing.

Maybe not. A hundred miles past Loach intersection, well out over the Labrador Sea, I'm watching Hinton in loose formation when suddenly, his P-38 banks sharply away from us. Not good, I speculate.

Sure enough, he has a problem with the right engine. Pumps, tanks, and mixtures don't help, and within about one minute, we collectively decide to abort. Our flight of three makes a sweeping right turn, and we begin tracking back toward Goose Bay.

Fortunately, Steve manages to keep things running and lands normally on two engines in Goose Bay. Hinton, Cardin, and our support team swing into action, and within an hour, they discover a cracked cylinder on the right Allison V1710. Lewis elects to change out both engines, and that's the end of the trip for the P-38. (After

Glacier Girl after the renovation. Photo courtesy of EAA

a double-engine change, Hinton will later return to Goose and fly the P-38 to EAA AirVenture Oshkosh.)

Within a few hours, we're mounted up again with Hinton riding with us in the Pilatus and Shipley formed on our right wing. The crossing to Narsarsuaq, Greenland, goes without a hitch in 3 + 10, we refuel both airplanes and continue on to Reykjavik, Iceland, in another 3 + 20, arriving at 0200 local.

As it turns out, most of the British Isles were suffering from a hellacious rain event, and the trip on down to Stornoway, Scotland, and Duxford, England, is delayed again. As much as I love Iceland (the best kept secret in the North Atlantic), there's no logical reason for me to hang out in Reykjavik. I jump on an Iceland Air flight to New York, then Delta back to California. It's my 173rd crossing of the North Atlantic.

Lyle Shelton's Search for Ultimate Speed

Here's how one pilot set the world prop/piston speed record and came to dominate Unlimited air racing.

If you're determined to make an airplane fly faster, traditional wisdom suggests there are three ways to realize that goal. In ascending order of difficulty: increase the power, improve the aerodynamics, or reduce the weight.

Perhaps no class of airplanes exemplifies the need for speed more than Unlimited air racers, and few pilots have pursued the quest for ultimate velocity as much as ex-Navy aviator Lyle Shelton.

When Lyle opted to build a competitive Unlimited air racer in the late 1960s, he attacked all three problems — on a budget. Unfortunately, but inevitably, Unlimited air racing is a rich man's sport, and Lyle had no bottomless pit of cash. He became an airline pilot after his military service, but even that salary wasn't adequate to feed the Unlimited race plane's voracious demand for money.

He also hoped to launch an assault on the world 3-kilometer prop/piston speed record, another extremely expensive project. At the time, the record was 469 mph, set by a German Messerschmitt Me 209 back in 1939.

Lyle was aware that fellow Reno Unlimited air racer Darryl Greenamyer was planning an assault on the record in his modified World War II Bearcat, exactly the type of airplane Lyle hoped he could push past 500 mph.

Sure enough, Greenamyer posted four 3-kilometer runs that averaged 483 mph in late summer 1969 and brought the world prop/piston speed record to the U.S.

Lyle chose the tiny Compton Airport in the middle of the LA Basin as home for his race plane buildup. With only 3,300 feet of runway, the uncontrolled Compton might seem an unlikely location for a WWII fighter project, but the rent was cheap, and Lyle's budget was small.

In 1968, Lyle moved a truck and trailer full of mangled airplane parts into the hangar next to mine at Compton, including what I guessed to be a Pratt & Whitney R-2800 radial engine.

As I helped him unload the pieces of airplane into his hangar, Lyle explained that these were the remains of a Bearcat that had crashed during an air show several years before in Valparaiso, Indiana. The airplane had been on short final to the airport when a horse ran out in front of it, and the pilot initiated a go-around.

Unfortunately, the new owner/pilot had no formal warbird experience other than a cockpit checkout and a few short hops in the single-seat fighter. He firewalled the throttle on the 2,250-hp engine, the airplane responded with a hard-left torque roll and crashed inverted on the edge of the runway.

Amazingly, the pilot survived, but the airplane was pretty much totaled. The wreck sat in a heap for several years in the tall brush of the airport, until Lyle heard about it and bought what was left after nearly a decade of weathering and cannibalizing.

Lyle was not without credentials in low-level flying. He was a former West Texas crop-duster and carrier pilot with time in a variety of jet fighters and attack aircraft, the latter including the king of all single-engine, piston-driven, ground-pounders, the Douglas A-1 Skyraider.

Lyle had also flown other pilots' Mustangs and Hawker Sea Furies at various racing venues but had a dream of someday building the world's fastest prop-piston airplane, an Unlimited racer that could dominate the competition.

Lyle knew the stock Bearcat was already one of the quickest machines flying behind pistons. He reasoned that an engine upgrade from the stock, P&W R-2800 to the Skyraider's Wright R-3350 powerplant might provide just the power he needed to win the gold at Reno, Miami, and the other race locations.

With very little money and an all-volunteer crew, that's exactly what he did. Miraculously, the Bearcat was in semi-flyable condition by September of 1969, and Lyle raced at Reno the same month, finishing a creditable fifth in a field of eight.

Over the next 35 years, I became an unpaid member of Lyle's crew, providing photographic support, feature stories, press releases, and whatever else I could do for Lyle's shoestring operation.

I watched Lyle and his mechanics transform and improve the airplane, eventually named Rare Bear, to a highly tuned, dramatically modified version of the original warbird. The team scavenged parts from everywhere — spares from other F8F owners and wrecked Bearcats, aircraft salvage yards, and overseas air forces where the Bearcat was still in military service. Lyle also bought/borrowed a number of junked DC-7 engines in hopes of assembling one that might actually run.

The Wright R-3350 engine was famous for its power but had thousands of moving parts and suffered from poor reliability in military service. TBO on the early models was about 100 hours, and even the later, improved versions only managed a 400-hour interval between overhauls. The powerful Wright engine was fitted to Boeing B-29s in WWII, was prone to overheating, and had a nasty habit of catching fire during long, Pacific bombing missions to Japan. Still, it was perfection from hell for those seeking high power at any cost.

Adapting the double-row, 18-cylinder Wright radial to fit the Bearcat was a demanding task, and fitting the airplane with a giant, four-blade, DC-7 propeller made Lyle's F8F a permanent tailwheel machine. The blades were so large that Lyle's modified fighter had to be flown off and back onto the ground in a three-point attitude to avoid a prop strike.

Given enough power, you could probably blast the Queen Mary into orbit, but Lyle was willing to settle for double the P&W's motive force. More accurately, the stock Pratt put out 2,250 hp, and the big Wright supernova-on-a-leash

Photo by Bill Larkins

employed 550 additional cubic inches to generate nearly 4,000 hp. Add water injection and nitrous oxide, and you might see as much as 4,500 hp — for a very short time.

The problem was/is that drag increases as the square of speed, and power required increases disproportionately. Lyle knew power alone wouldn't get him to his goal of 500 mph.

As a result, Lyle's crew incorporated a long list of aerodynamic improvements, most notably clipping a whopping 4 feet from each wingtip; replacing the large, stock, wraparound canopy with a smaller, more aerodynamic shape; and reducing intersection drag at the critical wing-root leading edge dramatically. There were myriad other minor changes to Rare Bear, all intended to improve the drag signature.

Lyle was always amazed at what his crew could accomplish on very little budget and short notice. He used to tell anyone who'd listen that "the pilot is the least valuable member of the ground crew," but in fact, Lyle was actually proficient at turning wrenches.

Reducing any airplane's weight is a trick even David Copperfield on his best day would be challenged to duplicate. Some of the aerodynamic improvements helped lower Rare Bear's empty weight, but the major contributors to speed were unquestionably the massive introduction of power and the major drag reduction.

The Bear was a work in progress for the next half century, but when the initial iteration was completed in 1969, the airplane weighed in at 8,700 pounds in race trim, and it flew with 4,500 hp. That's less than 2 pounds per horsepower, the lowest power loading I've heard of among Unlimited race planes.

The result of Lyle's modifications and improvements was indeed a record-setting machine. In 1972, Lyle took his F8F to Thermal, California, and established a new world time-to-climb record for prop/piston aircraft, high jumping from brake release to 3,000 meters (9,843 feet) in 91.9 seconds. That's a climb rate of 6,475 fpm, nearly the same as a Lear 23.

Rare Bear's power and speed made it a frequent winner on the air racing circuit, as well. Between 1972 and 1988, Lyle scored eight first-place Gold victories and four second-place Silver finishes.

In 1989, Lyle flew an NAA-approved, 3-kilometer course in Las Vegas, New Mexico, in hopes of capturing the world prop/piston speed record, then held by Steve Hinton in a P-51 Mustang at 499 mph. The crew had the Bear running perfectly, and Lyle made two low-level, two-way runs at an average speed of 528.33 mph, confirming Rare Bear, officially, as the fastest piston-powered airplane above the planet.

Lyle's record stood for 28 years, but in September 2017, Steven Hinton, Steve Hinton's son, edged past Rare Bear's record. The younger Hinton flew a P-51 named Voodoo and posted a speed of 531 mph.

Rare Bear went on to win six more Reno Gold races and finish second four times, making it the most successful Unlimited racer in the history of Unlimited air racing. In 2006, oilman Rod Lewis of San Antonio, Texas, purchased Rare Bear from Lyle for $2 million, and John Penney became its pilot. It hasn't raced since 2015.

Lyle Shelton died in 2010 at age 72, but it's unlikely his racing record will ever be surpassed. In a life dedicated almost exclusively to the pursuit of speed, Lyle could never afford to do everything he wanted with his Bearcat, yet he still somehow managed to win more races and set more records than anyone else in the world's fastest motor sport.

Record-Setting Mooney

Author holds speed records
that have stood for decades.

Photo by ©Ryan Scottini

Three-hundred mph — just a number, right? It does have a certain ring to it, though, doesn't it? Even today, when more manufacturers and pilots think in terms of knots, 261 knots doesn't sound nearly as impressive.

Not many general aviation airplanes flying behind piston engines will do it. In fact, no current piston-production airplane can manage it — one, two, or six engines. (There are one or two homebuilts capable of busting 300 mph, but only after you spend two to five years building them.)

Perhaps surprisingly, the airplane that comes closest is a single. It's Mooney's impressive TLS/Bravo/Acclaim S. Blessed with 270 hp, a turbocharger, and some of the slickest aerodynamics in the business, the TLS manages a quick 223 knots (256 mph) up at 25,000 feet. With the help of only about 40 knots of wind, the TLS could knock off 300 mph.

With speed like that on tap, wouldn't it be a kick to take advantage of late-winter westerlies and fly a Mooney TLS for some city-to-city world speed records? Since its introduction in 1989, the TLS has been unchallenged as the quickest machine of its kind, a natural to knock off whatever records exist in its weight category against any production airplane.

Setting world speed records, however, isn't simply a matter of choosing the fastest airplane. There are a number of considerations that can complicate such attempts. Official requirements, however, aren't among them. Here in the United States, all point-to-point record attempts are sanctioned by the National Aeronautics Association (NAA), the American division of the 80-nation governing body of aviation, the Fédération Aéronautique Internationale (FAI), based in Paris.

The NAA makes it relatively easy to comply with the regulations for record-setting. Pretty obviously, all applicants for record sanctions must be licensed pilots with current medical and biennial certificates. They must also be members of NAA and hold an FAI sporting license. The NAA provides the applicant with time-crossing-fix and time-of-departure/arrival forms to be filled out by the approach/center controllers or tower chiefs at the appropriate airports for point-to-point records. These are returned to the NAA to verify records claims.

On stock, production aircraft, the NAA accepts the manufacturer's weight and balance calculations (or the most recent Form 337) to qualify for the weight category. Experimental or tanked airplanes must be weighed fully fueled and loaded prior to the flight. When all fees are paid, the weight and balance numbers are approved, and all other paperwork is complete, you're off to the races.

Planning for my world speed records actually began more than a year before. Though then-Mooney President Jacques Esculier and national sales manager Jeff Dunbar were enthusiastic about the project, they were also adamant that any record I set be in a totally stock airplane. The point they wanted to make was that all Mooney

TLSs go like hell, not just the one I happened to be flying. Anyone willing to pay the fees, do the planning, and wait for the winds could set a record. In other words, I'd have to fly the records with a standard airplane, with only the TLS's 89-gallon tanks to protect me from evil. Esculier and Dunbar also wanted the records to be made coast-to-coast, with two major city pairs included.

Not a problem, I agreed, though it would mean I'd need to stop once for fuel. If I waited until January, February, or March, when the jet stream swung far enough south to provide some push, I just might make 261 knots (the magic 300 mph), even including the stop.

I looked at several routes and finally came up with one that met our mutual requirements. I chose Los Angeles, California, to Jacksonville, Florida, by way of Albuquerque, New Mexico, and Dallas, Texas. The LAX-ABQ-DFW-JAX route would allow me to fly coast-to-coast with only one stop if I got the winds I needed.

The great circle route suggested I'd practically have to overfly Albuquerque anyway, and there was an existing record for that leg that I could beat practically at idle power (151 knots set by an F33A Bonanza in 1990). Dallas was also nearly inline with Jacksonville, so I decided to zip across the top of DFW for the LAX-DFW record and land at Dallas Love Field (DAL) for fuel.

After what I hoped would be the fastest aircraft pit stop in history at Aviall on Dallas Love Field, it would be on to Jacksonville. Total great circle distance for the transcontinental record was 1,870 nm, though I'd be flying more like 1,890 nm to pass over Albuquerque and Dallas. If all went as planned and ATC accepted my GPS-generated flight plan, I'd set eight point-to-point world speed records, four in each of two classes, CIC and Unlimited: LAX-ABQ, LAX-DFW, LAX-JAX, and DAL-JAX.

I contacted Art Greenfield of the NAA to check on the route and sanction availability. The NAA grants only one 90-day sanction at a time for a given route and, if your preferred route is already taken, you'll either have to find another one or wait for the existing sanction to expire. If you choose the latter option, you may have a new, higher record to beat.

The world-record airplane, N9170R, was heavily equipped with all the options you'd expect in an aircraft designed to demonstrate (about the only options missing were TKS ice protection system and EFIS), but it was purely stock in all mechanical respects. The aircraft had the big, 116-cubic-foot oxygen bottle, capable of keeping two people breathing normally for seven hours at 25,000 feet.

From the outset, I knew I'd need really healthy winds just to make the first leg to Dallas. According to my Garmin GPS 100 AVD, LAX to DFW is a lengthy 1,071 nm, well outside the TLS's no-wind range at any published cruise-power setting.

There wouldn't be much point in flying a world speed record at less than max cruise, so I wouldn't reasonably have the option of coming back to long-range power. On the other hand, I agreed with Mooney that I'd use the standard 32/2400 cruise-power setting.

The plan was to depart Long Beach, California, and climb as high as possible before reversing direction, crossing the Los Angeles VOR to start the clock and heading toward Albuquerque GPS-direct. My ideal flight plan was to depart Long Beach and climb to 25,000 feet over the Pacific Ocean west of Los Angeles, then, reverse direction and come screaming back across LAX on course at full cruise with the wind at my back.

Unfortunately, I couldn't afford the fuel for a full climb to FL250 before turning east toward the VOR, so I planned to cross the VOR at 15,000 feet. I'd need at least a 33-knot average tailwind at FL250 just to make Dallas Love with the minimum seven-gallon reserve.

Weather was a major concern, partially because bad weather often accompanies good winds. Though I'd be filed IFR, I wanted the smoothest ride I could find to ensure the highest speed, which meant staying out of the clouds as much as possible to avoid icing conditions that generally go hand-in-hand with the jet stream and to avoid an instrument approach into Dallas. Though I didn't expect weather problems in Los Angeles other than the typical low-lying morning clouds and fog, thunderstorms are always a concern in central Texas in winter.

The GPS-direct route was another major source of concern. ATC bends over backward to accommodate record flights and because there's not much traffic at altitudes in the middle 20s, direct routings are pretty common. But I had no guarantee I'd be granted that privilege, and any deviation from a GPS-direct route would obviously extend the distance and reduce my average speed.

For navigation on the record hops, I planned to use multiple GPS units cross-checked against area navigation latitude/longitude waypoints. Primary GPS would be the aircraft's BendixKing KLN 90A, recently approved for en route IFR. The King unit was to be supplemented by my Garmin GPS 100 AVD, and two other Garmin portable systems. The KNS 81 would handle the area nav waypoints nicely as a double-check on GPS. I'd also carry two portable VHF communications radios, a King KX-99, and a Narco HT 870 in case of electrical failure. Since all Mooney TLSs come standard with two batteries and alternators, a complete electrical power loss was extremely unlikely.

Naturally, we wanted to maximize our speed by waiting for the most favorable jet stream winds. Windows of opportunity were fleeting — often no more than 12 hours long. I knew forecasting could also be fickle, so I learned to trust winds-aloft pilot reports and actual balloon soundings rather than forecasts.

My co-pilot for my world-record attempt was a pilot who understood GPS and turbos, had flown several Mooneys and other aircraft, and had also flown the length and breadth of the continent several times. Her job throughout the trip would be to monitor fuel and oxygen consumption, keep track of our times over the various checkpoints, and double-check me on navigation.

Our opportunity came during what was to be the last storm of the season. On March 24, the jet stream swung down and settled over the entire southern United States, bringing rain, turbulence, thunderstorms, and icing conditions to the Southwest. Winds at FL250 were forecast on the tail at velocities ranging from 80 to 110 knots. My kind of weather.

We launched from Long Beach at 6:25 a.m. on March 25, 1994, climbed to 15,000 feet over the Pacific Ocean off the California coast, and crossed back over the LAX VOR at exactly 14:48:40 Greenwich. As we turned northeast, the King KLN 90A and three backup GPSs all confirmed that the forecast winds were accurate. The airplane was already pushing 260 knots in the climb. The Los Angeles Basin was between waves of the storm, and we were able to barely top the clouds climbing through 24,000 feet without picking up ice. I leveled at FL250, set power at 32/2400 and 18 gph to keep the engine cool and the GPS's CDI centered.

Within a few minutes, our groundspeed leaped to a spectacular 315 knots (362 mph), nearly 90 knots on the tail. During the next hour, our speed touched 334 knots (384 mph) before dropping below 300 knots at the Arizona/New Mexico border.

As we approached Albuquerque, ATC advised of a flight of two U.S. Air Force F-111s coming the opposite direction almost head-on at FL240. With help from center, I picked them up at 8 miles and watched as we converged at a closing speed of nearly 1,000 mph. They screamed by below us at what seemed an incomprehensible speed and wagged their wings in "Hello."

We crossed Albuquerque International at 16:48:32, eight seconds under two hours even for 589 nm, according to the primary GPS. We'd averaged 294.5 knots (338.7 mph) for the first leg, nearly doubling the existing record.

Through some careful flight testing and wind analysis prior to our flight, I'd determined that the fastest descent profile into Dallas from 25,000 feet was a pushover to 500 fpm down at a predetermined point (in order not to lose too much of the prevailing tail wind up high), then, an increase to 1,200 fpm down at 18,000 feet and a final pushover to a maximum 2,000 fpm at 12,000 feet. I hoped to cross DFW at 3,000 feet or less, ATC permitting. During the descent, I called Dallas Love clearance delivery and picked up our incredibly simple outbound DAL-JAX IFR clearance. "Cleared GPS-direct. Maintain flight level 250."

We sped across the top of the giant DFW complex at 18:35:36, giving us an average speed of 283.7 knots (326.3 mph) for the 1,071 nm from LAX to DFW.

The controller expedited our arrival into Dallas Love, and Aviall was waiting with two hoses deployed. Our time on the ground was an amazingly short 12 minutes, and we leapt back into the air and lofted up to FL250 for the quick trip to Jacksonville.

The jet stream pattern had prepared me for less wind on the second leg where the jet stream typically begins to turn left, more north, and sure enough, the wind was down to an average 50 knots on the tail for the DAL-JAX hop. Ground speed ran between 265 and 280 knots for most of the 788 nm trip across the Gulf Coast to Jacksonville.

The tower was well-advised of our record attempt and approved a max speed low pass above Runway 07. Again, I stayed high as long as possible, then descended at high vertical speed to about 100 feet above the runway and flashed by the tower with airspeed well into the yellow. The controller confirmed I was running at nearly 300 mph pulling out of that final dive.

Time for the DAL to JAX leg was 3:02:24. That provided an average speed of 259.2 knots (298.1 mph) on the final leg.

Total time from coast to coast was 7:09:20 for 1,870 nm, an average 261.3 knots or 300.5 mph. We'd met my promise to Mooney of flying the world's fastest, piston-powered, production airplane at more than 300 mph from coast to coast, flying from Pacific to Atlantic at more than 300 mph (barely), and setting all eight of the records we'd planned for, four in weight class C1C and four more in Unlimited.

When last we checked, our quartet of C1C records still stood. It's unlikely anyone is liable to break them unless they have the combination of ingredients we had: an extremely fast airplane and excellent tailwinds.

Beach Azkorri (or Gorrondatxo)
in Getxo town, Biscay, Basque
Country, Spain.

Fine Whine

**Miscellaneous ramblings on contract flying
in Europe in a Piper turboprop.**

*Since long before airplanes blotted the
skies over Europe, bringing first bombs
and later tourists, the land itself has
represented the eternal truth.*

If speed is aviation's ultimate excess, altitude is its great equalizer. Fly high enough, and the sky below washes the Earth clean of the soiled hand of man, hiding the blemishes inflicted in the short span of a few hundred years. Even if you're flying low, altitude helps smooth out most of the wrinkles, softening the hard lines of age, leaving the face of the land peaceful and unspoiled.

Twenty-seven thousand feet is a good compromise, more than enough but less than too much, especially if you happen to be cruising effortlessly above Northern Spain in a Piper Cheyenne III propjet. From 5 miles tall in skies as clear as Chablis, you can see forever, or at least you can see the land that helped spawn 2,500 years of recorded history, which is close enough. This is most legitimately the Olde Country, though it's hard to tell from the high road. Take away cities and highways, and the Earth seems pristine and unspoiled — meadows without fences, rivers without bridges, roads without cars.

Directly below is the magnificent Basque Coast, beautiful, rugged geography rising straight out of the angry Atlantic, like Northern California with a Spanish accent. Somewhere down there — in fact, practically everywhere down there — thousands of privileged sheep graze the lush, placid hillsides of Asturias Province, unaware of my presence as I pass silently above them in the soft, yellow light of dawn.

Just over the horizon, beneath the quiet radiance of the new sun, France awakens to the early morning vineyard mists of fall. In Bordeaux and Pau and Toulouse and Perpignan, farmers prepare for yet another day of harvesting the grapes that produce arguably the world's finest wines.

Since long before airplanes blotted the skies over Europe, bringing first bombs and later tourists, the land itself has represented the eternal truth — the source of life for millions of people who haven't the slightest interest in Mach numbers, compressor rpm, or turbine inlet temperatures. Corporate travel by propjet may be something of an ultimate norm for a lucky few pilots, but the true people of the Earth, those who live by the land, will never know what they're missing and probably couldn't care less. For them, the heaven and the Earth comprise their sustenance, their world, their very life.

The sky is equally blasé about such technical accomplishments, but today it's also uncharacteristically cooperative, I muse, marveling at the visibility, watching the pointed white peaks of the Pyrenees materialize like armored knights in the distance. The mountains reach up for me, jealous of my artificial, man-made altitude, but fortunately, even their loftiest summits fall 3 miles short.

On the panel in front of me, I'm suitably impressed by the technology that allows me to fly so high and fast and protects me from evil. The DME and GPS argue the academic as to whether I am traversing Spain at 298 or 302 knots, and I wonder at all that passes below unnoticed in my haste. It seems somehow disrespectful that I should overfly so much history and tradition at nearly 5 miles a minute.

But time and business wait for no man, least of all a corporate pilot in a $2 million turboprop. I have been hired to help drive one of Piper's ultimate turbine twins around Europe for three weeks, a tough job, but …

Today, I am filed from Aviles to Barcelona, little more than a brief morning interval between breakfast and brunch in the big Cheyenne. I hurry southeast in my small, aluminum enclosure in the grip of an unseasonable high, shunted along by 30-knot tailwinds, floating on a column of sky as soft and smooth as an air mattress, which, in fact, it is. Outside, the atmosphere I transition is minus 35 degrees C, yet I luxuriate in 22 degrees inside my comfortable cabin, wondering how the other 98% lives.

Traveling through Europe by any private aircraft isn't nearly as tough as most pilots believe.
It's an aeronautical sightseer's paradise.

For those lucky enough to fly in Spain, there are few ways more comfortable than in Piper's big turbine, but traveling through Europe by any private aircraft isn't nearly as tough as most pilots believe. It's an aeronautical sightseer's paradise, and Spain offers some of the

There are few better ways to see Europe than in a $2 million Piper Cheyenne III. Photo by Adam Glowaski, Box5 Media (*box5media.com*)

best flying to be found on the continent. The people are friendly, the food is generally excellent, and the climate is good, especially south of Madrid where the atmospherics are closer to desert Casablanca than rainy Paris.

Still, many pilots have heard stories of terribly complex ATC procedures, universally rotten weather, perplexing language problems, high landing and parking fees, and a variety of other difficulties associated with operating in Europe.

Some of those stories are undoubtedly true. Logic doesn't always prevail in Europe any more than it does here in the U.S., but most stories are anecdotal exaggerations.

Whatever the level of simplicity or complication, there's little question that flying in Europe is more expensive than in the U.S. In 30 years of ferrying airplanes to foreign destinations as far flung as Japan, Australia, the Middle East, Europe, and Africa, I've rarely encountered problems that weren't at least partially of my own making. Pilots willing to do their homework and play by the rules will find Europe interesting and different, but more fun than challenging.

It's Not Easy Being Greenland

Flying in these parts, you're constantly aware of ice. It's worth the effort.

As I sit in Goose Bay watching the night-time snow fall and occasionally glimpsing the green/orange November glow of the aurora through breaks in the clouds, I can only dream of continuing across the ocean. Most of southern Greenland is down and out with fog and icing conditions, symptomatic of late fall.

If there's one absolute truth about flying the North Atlantic in a normally aspirated piston aircraft, it is ice. Those pilots who've been flying the ocean at low level for a few years recognize airframe icing as perhaps *the* most dangerous threat.

It doesn't matter much if your airplane is certified for icing. Standard pneumatic deice boots can give you a slight edge, and you probably have a little more advantage if your airplane is equipped with full "weeping wing" TKS, but icing is an equal-opportunity killer. In various forms, it has brought down airplanes of all sizes and descriptions, and it continues to account for two or three airplanes each year on the ferry run from Labrador to Greenland to Iceland to Europe.

As I sit in Goose Bay, watching the nighttime snow fall and occasionally glimpsing the green/orange November glow of the aurora through breaks in the clouds, I can only dream of continuing across the ocean. Most of southern Greenland is down and out with fog and icing conditions, symptomatic of late fall. So far, I've been stuck for four days, waiting for a break in weather, listening to the occasional wolf howl in the local forest and enjoying the crisp, minus 10 degrees Celsius weather.

On this trip, I'm flying a Marchetti SF.260, an Italian light-sport aircraft. Under normal conditions, the Marchetti is a brilliant aerobatic airplane, previously used by dozens of foreign governments as an entry-level military trainer. In keeping with its Italian lineage, the Marchetti is an athletic performer, possessed of incredibly smooth handling. I'm also told its slick airfoil is notoriously intolerant of icing in any form. I'd rather not find out about that.

The Marchetti comes standard with small fuel tanks everywhere (four altogether): a pair of 11-gallon, main-wing containers, and two 18-gallon tip tanks. I have an additional 32 gallons of ferry fuel installed behind me in what would normally be the kid's seat, but the placard limits that tank to 80% capacity or 26 gallons. If I was feeling brave, I could go to the full 32 gallons and risk being slightly outside the aft CG limit. I've flown airplanes beyond the aft limit before. I'm no longer that brave (or stupid, you choose one). This brings total fuel to 84 gallons. At a burn of 14 gph, I'd have six hours to exhaustion.

The leg across the Labrador Sea to Narsarsuaq, Greenland, is 680 nm, four hours at the Marchetti's typical 170-knot cruise. In other words, I have a two-hour reserve, not much in the Far North. It had better be enough. It would be difficult to fit the SF.260 with more fuel as the left passenger seat is filled to the roof with survival gear, charts, emergency rations, bottled water, and my one concession to comfort — a CD player. Flying diagonally across the U.S. from Santa Monica, California, to Bangor, Maine, and on to Goose Bay, the sounds of Bergeron, Goodwin, Kubis, Ferguson, and Kenton have helped keep me awake.

But for now, I wait for Greenland to freeze over, a phenomenon that occurs each fall/winter in mid-November. Narsarsuaq, my next destination, is near the coast, 42 miles up the narrow, winding Tunulliarfik Fjord, so its proximity to the Labrador Sea means it rarely experiences temperatures below about minus 15 degrees Celsius.

Colder is better, however. As the air gets colder, it becomes drier and for that reason, super-cooled water droplets are less likely to stick to an airplane wing in extreme low temperatures.

If Greenland becomes cold enough, I hope to cross at 5,500 feet with the help of tailwinds, land in Greenland just long enough to refuel and relaunch for Reykjavik, taking maximum advantage of the sparse five hours of daylight. With luck, I hope to be off Narsarsuaq early enough to clear the southern tip of Greenland while I can still see it, then fly straight to Iceland below the clouds.

I've been caught by the ice several times, mostly on this route, and it's always a problem when the limit of your deicing equipment is pitot heat. The worst instance was in a new but relatively defenseless Piper Archer some 25 years before. I was headed from Vero Beach to Genoa, Italy, heavily tanked and easily capable of making the direct 1,350 nm hop from Goose Bay to

Reykjavik without having to stop in Greenland. That meant I could avoid the island continent's super-expensive fuel, in those days $8 per gallon (now $17 per gallon). In this case, that was a good thing, as the weather was characteristically bad in both Godthab, Greenland's capitol, and Narsarsuaq.

I was tracking across the NDB at Prins Christian Sund on Greenland's south tip when I got caught in a band of icing that seemed to go on forever. Within a few minutes, it became obvious the only way out was down before the ice deformed the wing so badly that I'd lose control. I descended from 9,000 feet, dropped out of the bottom of the clouds at 500 feet above the Atlantic, and continued down to about 100 feet above the waves, where the temperature was barely 1 degree Celsius. It took a half-hour for the ice to sublimate, as I droned on toward Reykjavik, watching the angry Atlantic rolling 20 feet at the crests just below me.

If you ever need to appreciate your insignificance on the face of the planet, the Davis Strait between Greenland and Iceland at 100 feet is a great place to study. I stayed at that altitude all the way to Iceland, then ATC forced me to pull up into the ice clouds again to shoot the ILS approach into Reykjavik.

Fast forward to the Italian Marchetti trip. After nearly a week of waiting in Goose, I called my friends at Halifax FIC and was given the news I hoped I wouldn't have to hear. Greenland would be down for at least another week, possibly two.

Accordingly, I called the client in East Midlands, England, and suggested he'd save money by sending me home to California rather than pay my daily rate to babysit the Marchetti in Goose Bay with nowhere to go. Fortunately, he agreed, and I was on the next Air Canada jet to Halifax, then on to Toronto, and finally home to Los Angeles the following morning.

After perhaps 30 trips through and over Greenland, I've learned a thing or three about flying there. If the weather is down, I'll often use the infamous "up-the-fjord" approach that winds in toward Narsarsuaq from the North Atlantic. The fog sometimes makes that a challenge, but the alternative is to divert north to Godthab (now renamed Nuuk). Sadly, if Narsarsuaq is unflyable, Godthab usually is as well.

Over the years, the path leading to BGBW, the airport code for Narsarsuaq, has collected several airplanes on the bottom of its fjord, virtually all trying to sneak up into the airport.

As a result, that ad-libbed, semi-VFR procedure has been declared illegal, subject to a fine and other penalties. As a result, you now must pull up into the ice and shoot the extremely dangerous instrument approach over the mountains and down into the seashore surrounding the airport.

10

Eyjafjallajökull is still an active volcano, though it doesn't erupt very often and hasn't since this 2010 event.

Flying on Ice

In the Far North, ice can be a hazard both above *and* below.

It's often called the land of fire and ice, but for much of the year Iceland lives up to only part of that nickname. Perched far north on the upper right corner of the North Atlantic, a mere 100 miles south of the Arctic Circle, Iceland is regarded as one of Europe's best-kept secrets.

Despite its elevated latitude, the small country enjoys a surprisingly temperate arctic climate, and for pilots, that presents the possibility for in-flight icing virtually year-round.

Occasionally, however, another geologic/weather factor confuses Iceland's atmospherics — a volcanic eruption. It is late May 2010, and Eyjafjallajökull, a volcano in eastern Iceland, has been erupting for two months. Persistent, strong westerly winds have pushed a huge ash cloud southeast, grounding aircraft all across Europe and Scandinavia.

The same winds have stranded me at Reykjavik's Hotel Loftleidir, right on the city's downtown airport. I snuck in from Shannon, Ireland, a week ago, skirting around the ash cloud on the western side.

As I look out onto the parking ramp directly below, "my" '58 Baron wears a white sport coat of light snow in mid-May. Today, the folks at Iceland weather promise the prevailing westerlies should abate from their six-day average of 40-50 knots to more like 20 knots.

I'm planning to fly to Kulusuk on Greenland's magnificent, fjord-locked east coast; refuel with $17 per gallon avgas, then hop across the ice cap to Sondre Stromfjord on the opposite coast. Conditions permitting, I'll top off once again and continue across the Labrador Sea to Iqaluit, Nunavut, Canada — 1,200 nm total.

Though the legs on the North Atlantic milk run route aren't long, my airplane isn't tanked or deice-equipped, and weather is always a major concern that far north, partially because of the lack of alternates.

In-flight icing can be nearly ever-present north of 60 degrees latitude, and much of the time that means flying beneath an ice-filled overcast, even in spring.

I low-jump out of Reykjavik, point the nose west and level a few minutes later at 6,000 feet, barely below the overcast. Looking down from less than a mile above the Denmark Straits on my leg from Reykjavik to Kulusuk, Greenland, I try not to think about the minus 2 degrees Celsius water below and the icebergs that help keep it that cold.

Icebergs aren't exactly my friends, but I keep track of their positions just in case. They're definitely not miniature emergency landing strips but could serve as possible refuge in case I had to ditch in salt water chilled well below freezing. Provided I did everything right during the ditching, my dry suit and raft/paddle might provide the edge I'd need to make it to a berg and get out of the water. After that, the odds of survival improve slightly if a dozen other "ifs" are satisfied.

One hundred miles west of Reykjavik, I spot what appear to be breaking waves below, but after a minute or two I realize they're not what they seem.

In the maritime world, these are called growlers — solid white icebergs often mistaken for the whitecaps of ocean waves. These display a minuscule portion of their mass above water but hide huge, inverted ice mountains below.

Growlers are especially dangerous to ships navigating these waters because they're rock-hard new ice floating south with the current. A cursory scan with binoculars might suggest they're simply harmless breakers, but breakers eventually dissolve into open ocean. Growlers maintain their shape and sometimes surprise ship's captains by holing the hull of anything less sturdy than an ice breaker.

As I approach Greenland, the ice fields below become more consistent but less distinct, and the overcast drops lower. I'm forced to descend below the MEA, 5,500 feet, but Iceland control seems unconcerned, probably because there's not a lot of traffic at low altitude between Iceland and Greenland, and even if there was, there's no radar available to help keep it separated.

The visibility diminishes, though I still have ground contact, or in this case, water/ice contact, below. Twenty miles from Kulusuk, ac-

There are growlers in the water near Jökulsárlón glacier.

cording to Mr. Garmin, I realize I've become the victim of an insidious white out. I've probably been staring straight at the ice cap for some time, but everything is white: the sky above, the ice below, and Greenland itself.

I land on the gravel runway in Kulusuk, Greenland, refuel, and head for Sondre Strom, a former U.S. air base on the opposite side of the frozen continent. Operating several hundred pounds under gross now, the Baron rockets through the overcast with predictable rime icing, and I pop out on top at 8,000 feet. The ice cap 10 miles ahead continues sloping uphill to 10,000 feet then becomes a flat mattress of snow stretching to the horizon in three directions.

Level at 12,500 feet VFR, it's hard to believe Greenland is actually a mountain catch basin that has gradually filled with two miles of ice and snow over the millennia. At its grandest, the island continent measures 500 miles wide and 800 miles tall, from Nanortalik at the bottom to Knug Rasmussen Land at the top, near 85 degrees latitude and less than 600 nm from the North Pole.

Today, weather on Greenland's west coast is clear, so Sondre Strom is wide open. That's fortunate, as Godthab to the south and Thule to the north would both be stretching range on the Baron.

There are no longer any operational radio nav aids on top of the ice cap, but there is one abandoned distant early warning (DEW) line

The settlement of Kulusuk has never had more than a few hundred inhabitants.

station that offers a VFR checkpoint roughly on course between Kulusuk and Sondre Strom. Code-named "Sob Story," the giant, golf-ball
shaped, geodesic radar dome was abandoned many years ago, along
with its two similarly configured radar stations, Big Gun and Sea Bass.
In those dangerous Cold War days of the '70s and '80s, DEW line stations used to scan north looking for Russian bombers trying to sneak
over the pole to North America.

Imagine being stationed at Sob Story, perched on the ice at 10,000
feet MSL, with nothing but snow and sky for hundreds of miles in every direction.

Back in the late '70s and early '80s, when I was transiting back and
forth to Europe on a regular basis, I used to call up the poor souls
stationed on those bleak outposts and ask for a check of my exact position and groundspeed. The frequencies for the DEW line stations were
supposed to be secret, but everyone knew how to reach them. This was
long before GPS, and ferry aircraft were rarely equipped with VLF/
omega, so position information was strictly point-and-shoot, sometimes assisted by non-directional beacons.

The airmen on duty at the DEW line stations were usually bored silly and happy to help; then they'd want to chat for as long as I was in range, asking about my airplane, my destinations, my home town, and anything else that might keep me talking. Apparently, there wasn't a lot to do at the DEW line facilities.

It's fairly apparent when you first spot Sondre Stromfjord, known by the locals as Kangerlussuaq, that the airport is a former U.S. air base. There are a number of huge hangars on the south side of the field, obviously designed to house C-130-style cargo aircraft. When equipped with skis, these helped resupply the radar stations on the ice cap. The weather at Sondre Strom Air Base is usually better than any southern Greenland airport, so regular ferry flights talked to the military controllers often.

Once, back in the '80s, I was returning from Amman, Jordan, to Fargo, North Dakota, with a cloud-seeding Beech Duke, and was talking to one of the controllers at the DEW line station nearest to Sondre Stromfjord. I asked him if he had a groundspeed on me and he replied almost instantly, "You're grounding at 180 knots."

"That's pretty good for a westbound flight at this time of year," I said. "Do you have any other nav information on my little airplane?"

After a short pause, he came back with, "Yes sir. Your heading to Goose Bay is 265 degrees, your altitude is 14,050 feet and your number three cylinder on your left engine is running a little hot."

I checked, and, no, it wasn't, but he was obviously incredibly bored and just making conversation.

11

Faroe Islands

Into the

Wind

Flying a semi-backwards ferry from Europe to California with my old nemesis, the wind.

I was awakened from a deep sleep by what sounded like sporadic repetition of "baaharalmminumm" (forgive my poor onomatopoetic translation). I mentally shake off the dream, park my red-and-white Ferrari SF-16H Formula One car after winning the Monaco Grand Prix, then fight my way back to consciousness. The sound repeats itself over and over.

Oh yes, now I remember. I'm in Vágar, Faroe Islands, a long, long way from Monaco. The strange sound seems to be practically in my room or perhaps just outside my ground level window.

Here in the sub-Arctic, the hotel's bottom floor is in the basement with windows that open out onto the "green," in this case more of a dirty gray, grass just beginning to recover from the Faroes' inhospitable winter.

I open the blinds of my one small window, and there, staring back at me, is a large, wooly sheep, chomping sideways on the grass stubble and obviously not especially impressed by the curious human before her.

I check the clock, and notice I'm about due to be up and out, anyway. It's 5 a.m., and the sun is already well above the horizon here in mid-May. It's time to check with flight service and see if I can sneak into Iceland against the giant westerly wind tunnel that seems to prevail much of the year on the North Atlantic.

Winds can be a consistent problem in this part of the world, especially on any westbound Atlantic hop above the high ocean.

The Faroe Islands perch far up north, well above the British Isles and the infamous North Sea. You might expect the weather in such a far-flung outpost to be little better than atrocious, and some of the time, you'd be correct.

You might expect the weather in such a far-flung outpost to be little better than atrocious, and some of the time, you'd be correct.

On this occasion, the weather has been reasonably clement, but the winds have been nothing less than horrific, and I had no choice but to visit Vágar for the overnight.

I'd probably made 80-100 trips on the Iceland-Scotland sky trail and had never had to divert before. The weather wasn't really that bad for the westbound ferry of a Cessna 340 from Germany to California, but the characteristic winds were howling across Greenland and Iceland, then swirling southeast toward the British Isles, as if replicating my exact course in reverse.

This is my first wintertime reverse ferry (as hardly anyone calls it anymore), flying "backwards" into gale force winds to the U.S. from points European. I've flown over the Faroes twice before, once en route to Helsinki, Finland, in a raggedy Navajo Chieftain, and the second time transiting from Iceland to Northern Germany in a Mirage. The islands always looked small and forbidding from 11,000 feet or above, but on this trip, I was forced to visit them at ground level.

My airplane this time is a Cessna 340 out of Dortmund, headed for Palo Alto, California, for a double-engine change at Victor Aviation. Like so many high-time engines, these two are running incredibly well, not producing much power but doing so very smoothly. Both engines have been holding hands for 1,900 hours, and the German owner had finally decided to spring for a pair of Victor Black Edition overhauls. He elected to do the job right and have the airplane ferried to Victor's shop in California. My kind of guy.

Most of the time, there's little reason to stop in Vágar (the only airport on these remote islands), westbound or eastbound. The Faroes are roughly halfway out on the leg from Scotland to Iceland, and the full distance is only 650 nm. Yesterday, however, the winds were wailing at 80 knots, slowing the Cessna twin to a groundspeed of about 100 knots.

The airplane is untanked, so I have six hours of fuel, not nearly enough, I decided, before I left Prestwick. I knew the atmospherics were agreeable as far as Vágar, and that would put me halfway to Reykjavik, Iceland, my usual stop.

I check out of the hotel, wave goodbye to my wake-up sheep, and stop by the weather office for the bad news. The man with the charts assures me that nothing has changed since yesterday and seems a little surprised that anyone would expect it to. Big winds, big waves, and a small window of opportunity to scamper into Iceland before the sky turns to ice. It's clear beneath the clouds, but still cold and inhospitable above 5,000 feet. The winds are more agreeable down low, so I elect to file VFR for the short hop northwest.

With nothing more than full fuel, me, and 80 pounds of luggage and survival gear to lift, I low-jump out of Vágar, climb to 4,500 feet and set course for VM, the first and only radio beacon on the way into BIRK, the ICAO identifier for Reykjavik.

The sheep apparently awakened the wind when she summoned me, and as predicted, I have about 40 knots on the nose. I point the airplane toward where Reykjavik used to be and settle in for the short 2-plus-20 trip.

No more than 30 minutes out, I spot a tiny sailboat tacking into the wind on the angry ocean below, almost invisible in the confusion of breaking waves and rolling surf. My God, I wonder, is he really sailing to Iceland in these winds? Anyone with that level of intestinal fortitude has to be saluted, I decide, so I make a race-track circle off to the side, losing altitude to 500 feet, and fly by the boat's starboard side, watching the insignificant little craft crashing through 10-foot waves.

The boat's captain, apparently the tiny craft's only occupant, waves his hat at me as I pass on the right. I wag my wings in recognition and make another 360 to come by him again, marveling at his ability to tack back and forth, 22 degrees to left and right of the wind, and still move forward.

Thirty years ago, when I thought learning to sail would make me more popular with women, I was equally mystified by the phenomena, both sailing and women. I learned a little about the former in the classroom of Long Beach Harbor; never did learn much about the latter.

Winds over the oceans have always been the nemesis of pilots because the consequences of a misjudgment can be severe. If you're flying over land and winds don't work out as forecast, you can simply punch the PTT button and say, "Center, Rocket Bird

3274B would like to divert to one of the 14 airports within 10 miles. Which do you recommend?" Out over the water, you often must make it to your original destination — or not.

Unlike the sea captain below who need not worry about fuel consumption (unless someone turns off the wind), most of us who fly these routes adopt strict rules about wind interpretation, fuel burn, and reserve, preferring to be living pessimists rather than optimists living on the edge.

First, we reduce any forecast tailwind by 10 knots and increase any headwind by at least 5 knots. Then, we assume that every ferry tank holds 3 gallons less fuel than the placard indicates (there's none aboard this airplane), and each wing tank's capacity is actually 2 gallons less than it's supposed to be. Finally, we build in at least a two-hour reserve on the Pacific and an hour and a half on the Atlantic.

As I circle one more time and give a good luck wing-waggle to the stalwart sailboat captain below, I can't help admiring his determination.

I cruise climb back up to 4,500 feet, punch up the altitude hold, and settle in for the last 1-plus-30 flight into Reykjavik.

If you have to be stuck somewhere on the North Atlantic, you couldn't possibly pick a better place than Reykjavik. I've been weathered-in there probably 50 times, and it's certainly one of the friendliest overnight stops anywhere in the world, even if overnight turns into two or three days, which it often does.

I never saw Reg Philmore again. I'd like to imagine he's somewhere out on a cold ocean, ignoring headwinds and smiling at bad weather, perhaps preparing to sail around the world from pole to pole.

Three days later while I'm waiting for civilized winds and weather in Greenland, I wander down to the harbor and spot the little sailboat tied up at the guest docks, looking none the worse for wear. I discover that the owner is a gentleman named Reg Philmore from Duxford, England, and that he's staying at the Loftleidir Hotel, where I'm also temporarily marooned.

We make contact, have dinner and I learn that while Reg is not a pilot, he's an enthusiastic follower of World War II airplanes. He lives in the right place, as Duxford is famous for one of the U.K.'s largest WWII museums: the Imperial War Museum. It's also home to one of the country's premier flying warbird displays: the Duxford Air Show.

The winds died down the following morning, and I flew to Kulusuk and Sondrestrom, Greenland, on over to Iqaluit, Nunavit, Canada, and down to Goose Bay for the overnight.

I never saw Reg Philmore again. I'd like to imagine he's somewhere out on a cold ocean, ignoring headwinds and smiling at bad weather, perhaps preparing to sail around the world from pole to pole.

12

Many of the "airports" in Africa are grass strips.

Memories of Africa

Part 1: The Risks and Costs of Flying in Africa
Part 2: Crash-Landing in the Middle of Nowhere
Part 3: Ferrying a Caravan
Part 4: Double Engine Failure

Part 1: The Risks and Costs of Flying in Africa

Africa has always had a certain indefinable attraction that not everyone understands. Over the years, I've delivered probably two dozen airplanes to the continent, with destinations including Egypt, Ethiopia, Djibouti, Kenya, Ivory Coast, Cameroon, Namibia, and South Africa.

Africa's rules of the air can be very different, and that's both good news and bad news. Much of the continent is relatively unsettled, and that means most of the time, no one will care how you fly — until they start shooting at you.

Africa's rules of the air can be very different, and that's both good news and bad news. Much of the continent is relatively unsettled, and that means most of the time, no one will care how you fly – until they start shooting at you.

Back in 1983, I was flying my first African trip with two other pilots who'd been across the politically volatile Sahara many times, and they both suggested the safest way was to fly at night, as high as possible, and with all lights off to avoid becoming the target of a 15-year-old with a shoulder-launched TOW missile. Regardless of the risk, I wasn't about to miss what I thought might be my only opportunity to see the

Sahara, despite dire predictions of possible AAA ground fire and sand-storms that often dropped visibility to less than a mile.

Eventually, my fellow pilots reluctantly agreed to fly the 2,000-nm leg from Funchal, Madeira Islands, to Abidjan, Ivory Coast, in daylight, but only if we all climbed to 13,000 feet (our mutual maximum height without supplemental oxygen) and stayed together. We did exactly that, the weather was perfect with 100-mile visibility, and we all arrived safely in Ivory Coast after a totally uneventful, 14-hour crossing.

A day later, a locust-suppression Douglas DC-6 was shot down by mistake in the Western Sahara. It was little consolation that the government found the young soldier who made the mistake and executed him on the spot.

Another ferry pilot wasn't as lucky as we were. He was ferrying a Turbo Arrow to South Africa and elected to fly down the east coast of the continent rather than taking the normal west coast route. With nothing but an occasional village below, he was flying low over the Tsavo National Park in southern Kenya, skimming along barely above the trees enjoying the animals and the scenery, when suddenly he hit something. The airplane immediately lost all power and crashed on the veld. The pilot was uninjured. Fortunately, his HF radio still worked, he got off a mayday and was picked up the following morning.

When the rescuers arrived, it was all too obvious what had happened. A few hundred yards behind the wrecked Turbo Arrow was a decapitated giraffe. The pilot was arrested and thrown in jail for hunting in a national park.

In one respect, the pilot was lucky. Search and rescue is a "sometimes" thing in Africa. Flying over countries where fast food is a gazelle and there's often no such thing as a stable government means there often are no resources remaining for SAR personnel or equipment. Standard advice when crossing the Gulf of Guinea (the notch in the south Atlantic along the west African coast) has always been to bring along a large paddle as well as the usual raft and vests. If you go down, you'd better know where you are and start paddling, as it's unlikely anyone will come looking for you. There simply aren't many search-and-rescue assets in most of Africa.

Money has always been a key to flying in Africa, and you'll pay a fee for practically everything. In Libreville, Gabon, the light fee used to be $96, charged to every airplane that took off at night, be it a 747 or a Super Cub. On one trip to South Africa in a gaggle of four airplanes, we stopped for the night in Libreville and were up well before dawn the next day for the next leg down to Windhoek, Namibia.

After the sun broke the eastern horizon, the slowest airplane, a Cherokee Six, departed while the rest of us had another cup of coffee. The universal advice in Africa was to plan arrival at the same time so we could split one customs call-out fee rather than pay individual fees.

As we were readying for departure a half-hour later, the airport jeep rolled up to the boss of the other ferry company, and the smiling official walked up to the pilot and said, "That will be an extra $96 for the light fee for your other pilot."

Ernie said, "No, I'm sorry. There must be some mistake. He didn't lift off until after the sun had risen. We all watched him."

The official maintained his wide grin and said, "You must pay the fee or your flight plan will not be approved."

Ernie lost it. Pointing at the huge ball of the sun, he shouted, "You see that. That's the sun. It's up."

The airport official never lost a beat. With the same big smile, he pointed at the runway and said, "You see those. They are runway lights. They are on."

Ernie paid.

Clearances are required to fly over much of Africa, but the governments often are so disorganized, there's no one available to grant a clearance. As a result, we often requested overflight clearances, were ignored for two or three days, then just went anyway, hoping we wouldn't need to land.

In one instance, I was bringing a Seneca II back from Johannesburg to Florida, and I was determined to fly up the center of Africa rather than traveling the same old west coast route. Predictably, no one answered my requests for clearances in the "Z" countries, Zimbabwe, Zambia, and Zaire (now Democratic Republic of Congo), so I just filed my paperwork and departed. Almost no one ever asked for a clearance number anyway, so I wasn't too worried.

Interestingly, of the two VORs and 13 NDBs I'd planned to use for navigation aids on the 1,600-nm leg to Libreville, not one was on the air. No big surprise. I flew low, well above giraffe height, at about 1,000 feet AGL, enjoying the view and navigating by a combination of pilotage and dead reckoning.

As I approached Kinshasa, Zaire, known to be in a perpetual state of revolution, I dialed up the appropriate approach control frequency to check for traffic. I called Kinshasa as a courtesy, and to my surprise, the controller came back and immediately asked for a clearance number.

In my best, deep, airline pilot voice, I said, "Roger, Kinshasa, stand by while I look it up."

After an appropriate pause to pretend I was finding the number, and once again summoning my most confident voice, I ad-libbed a non-existent clearance number, hoping I could bluff them just long enough to get across the Congo River to Brazzaville, Congo, while they checked it. "Kinshasa Control, November 3274 Bravo has clearance number 4679Echo-BravoSierra6459, issued in Victoria Falls, Zimbabwe, and dated 10/17/86."

In 20 years of flying Africa, I'm happy to have had the experience, and I'm even happier to have survived it.

After a few seconds, the controller came back with, "Roger November flight, your clearance checks, cleared to Brazzaville, Port-Gentil, Libreville, direct. Have a nice flight." It was obvious they had no way of actually checking a clearance, so if you sounded as if you knew what you were doing, they assumed you must be OK.

Africa seems to generate such experiences nearly automatically, and there are hundreds of other stories I could tell about flying in that unusual and sometimes beautiful place. In 20 years of flying Africa, I'm happy to have had the experience, and I'm even happier to have survived it.

Part 2: Crash-Landing in the Middle of Nowhere

April 18, 1998, Djibouti, Africa — As we load into the cab outside the hotel at 6:30 a.m., the sun is just boiling up above the eastern horizon. Hard by the Gulf of Aden, Djibouti is hot and wet all year round, perched on the Horn of Africa. Geographically sandwiched in the eastern Sahara between Eritrea, Ethiopia, Somalia, and the Gulf of Tadjoura, it is so hot so much of the time that the French Foreign Legion does its hot weather training there.

The ride to Djibouti/Ambouli Airport over half-paved roads seems interminable, and by the time we arrive at 7:15 a.m., the temperature is already pushing 38 degrees Celsius. Humidity is so intense, it's almost like walking through a fine sprinkler. Flying weather is what passes for clear; a haze that rolls in off the gulf and lingers nearly full time.

When we arrived last night, we had the huge ramp to ourselves. Overnight, a giant Russian Antonov AN-124, then the second-largest airplane in the world, arrived and now shadows our tiny Piper Lance. While the fueler begins to manually wobble-pump 100 octane (we hope) into our tanks from a trailer, I walk over to the behemoth and climb the ladder to the Antonov's cockpit to see if the flight crew has any weather for the flight south. The airport's weather office had only satellite photos. Sadly, the captain's English is little better than my Russian, so we mostly smile a lot, then shrug, shake hands, and part company.

This is the 14th and final leg on our 10,000-nm trip from Santa Monica, California, to Nairobi, Kenya. We departed California on April 7, flew diagonally across the U.S. to Bangor, Maine, on to Goose Bay, Labrador, Canada, delayed for two days to avoid blizzard conditions in Greenland, then made the jump to Reykjavik, Iceland, with a quick fuel stop in Narsarsuaq.

In the following days, it was on to Glasgow, Scotland, then Palma de Majorca, Spain, then Iraklion, Greece, on the island of Crete, and down to Luxor. As of today, we have spent 12 days on this trip, and I'm eager to complete the delivery and jet back to Los Angeles.

It takes nearly two hours to fill the Lance's 100-gallon ferry tank and 94-gallon wing tanks, then another half hour to argue with airport officials about fees and fuel costs. We're finally ready to fly at about 10:30, destination, Nairobi, or so we hope.

Just as on yesterday's leg from Luxor, Egypt, the Lance begins to overheat shortly after takeoff. Yesterday, we couldn't come anywhere near our filed altitude of 9,000 feet. We step-climbed for nearly an hour and finally advised Jeddah control that we'd need to make our final altitude 5,000 feet.

Jeddah wasn't happy about that, but we had little choice. As a result, center kept us out over the middle of the Red Sea until we entered Djibouti's airspace. Today, the temperature is even higher. Before pushing up power for takeoff, I note 43 degrees Celsius (110 degrees Fahrenheit) on the OAT. An inversion keeps the temperature uncomfortably high during the climb toward Dire Dawa VOR, the only navaid we'll utilize on our bumpy, 900-nm leg to Kenya.

Again, I step climb 1,000 feet at a time, monitoring the Lance's CHT right on the redline most of the time and, just as yesterday, I'm forced to level well below my planned 10,000 feet. Trouble is, this time, I'll need that altitude to clear the mountains of eastern Ethiopia. I'm hoping I can slowly milk the airplane up to 10,000 feet as I fly south and we burn down fuel.

We filled every tank in the airplane at Djibouti as a hedge against having to deviate to the east toward Somalia. We hope we don't have to do that, as there's no central government in Somalia and therefore no one to issue a clearance. Even if we had a clearance, the various rebel factions might take potshots at us just for fun.

Weather is about as good as it gets in this part of the world, puffy clouds offering broken to overcast conditions. I'm forced to dodge around the cumulus and occasional cumulonimbus buildups as we parallel the high country, gradually being pushed east toward Somalia.

The GPS suggests we are very near the Somali border, far left of course, but I have no choice. A combination of weather and terrain makes it inadvisable to fly the normal track. I advise Addis Ababa of the deviation on HF, and they respond with a totally disinterested, "Roger, good luck." Unlike the travelogues of other parts of Africa, there are no rivers and few trees below. We haven't seen any animals yet, probably because of the lack of water. I know there are few search-and-rescue resources in this part of the continent, so we'd better not have a problem.

As if on cue, we do. Five hundred miles out, as we traverse the Ogaden Desert approaching the border with Kenya, I sense rather than hear what seems a slight roughness. I put both hands on the yoke to check for vibration, and the engine indeed feels rougher.

Thirty seconds later, the big Lycoming emits a short BRRRRT, then coughs once and transitions to a regular rough. I watch as the No. 2 EGT drops off the bottom of the gauge. Number 2 is no longer firing.

Sure enough, within a minute or two, the regular "rough" turns ratty as pieces of the number two jug begin to destroy the other cylinders, and it's apparent we're going down.

I reverse direction toward a game trail I'd crossed a few minutes ago, knowing that things will probably get worse before they get better. Fuel pump on, switch tanks, adjust mixture, check mags, pray — nothing helps. Sure enough, within a minute or two, the regular "rough" turns ratty as pieces of the No. 2 jug begin to destroy the other cylinders, and it's apparent we're going down.

As I set up for the emergency landing, I'm aware that we are flying above terrain that redefines "the middle of nowhere." We haven't seen a village, a building or even a dirt road for at least an hour. This remote section of Africa is infamous as being totally without any form of government, no law, no military, no police protection, nothing.

I spiral down toward the craggy scrub brush below and aim for the only semi-clear area I can see, 700-800 feet of what appears to be flat desert interrupted by thorn bushes. Power is totally gone now.

As I line up on the touchdown point, I know this will not be fun.

The engine staggered and coughed as the Ogaden Desert rose to meet me. I'd tried everything to restore power and nothing worked. The Piper Lance's engine analyzer suggested the No. 2 cylinder had failed, and it was obviously determined to take the other five with it.

At 1,500 feet above the tortured terrain, it was apparent No. 2 had won, so I switched to survival mode. Where could I park the Lance without tearing it, and us, to pieces?

"Us," in this case, referred to owner, Thomas Jones, in the right front seat. Jones had hired me to find and buy this airplane, totally restore it, and then ferry it from California to Kenya with him as passenger. The first 13 hops across the North Atlantic, Europe, and the Middle East had gone well. This was the last leg of the trip, Djibouti to Nairobi, and we were nearly halfway there when the engine became ratty and finally quit.

Wheels up or wheels down, I wondered? The terrain below offered no real landing sites in a rugged, forbidding landscape of sand, rocks, and scrub brush. There was a narrow, curving game trail below, the only possible landing site, but it appeared to be bisected by deep ruts, anything but smooth. At 500 feet AGL, I put the gear down anyway to let it absorb some of the impact. If I got lucky and the ruts weren't as bad as they looked, I just might be able to slam it on and grind to a stop on a short section of straight dirt.

The wheels locked into place a hundred feet above the barren, craggy desert. Outside air temperature was well above 45 degrees Celsius as the airplane staggered through the broiling air above the Acacia thorn bushes.

The ruts were worse than they looked. The Lance's touchdown was gentle, but that was the last thing gentle about the landing. Within a few seconds, the right gear dropped violently into a foot-deep hole and departed the airplane, slamming the right wingtip to the ground. A half-second later, the left wheel caught in a rut and held, slewing the Piper hard left, breaking off the nose gear, chewing up the bushes and spewing sand high in the air.

It was all over in a few seconds, and we were out of the airplane and running for our lives the instant the Lance came to rest. We had a 100-gallon ferry tank directly behind us, still half full, and all I could think about was the possibility of fire.

It was all over in a few seconds, and we were out of the airplane and running for our lives the instant the Lance came to rest. We had a

100-gallon ferry tank directly behind us, still half full, and all I could think about was the possibility of fire.

Fortunately, the airplane didn't burn. After the dust settled, we stood in the heat, stunned by the enormity of our situation. Technically, my Garmin handheld GPS showed us at N04-48.7/E041-22.1. More realistically, we were 600 miles from the nearest major city, Addis Ababa. The village of Mandera, Kenya, was 60 air miles away, also the location of the nearest water. We were stranded in one of the driest places on Earth. Many residents here have never seen a rainbow because rainbows demand rain.

Looking in any direction, the view was monochromatic and endless, nothing but tan desert, brown brush, and an occasional black-hot hill, either five or 50 miles distant, no way to tell which. It was hard to believe anything lived here. There seemed to be no water and hardly any food, yet this part of east Africa was a haven for cobras, Acacia thorn bushes with inch-long spines, and other unpleasant life. In the Ogaden, if it didn't bite, stab, or sting, it was probably a rock.

I had my portable communication radio with me, and Thomas wondered if anyone would hear a transmission on 121.5 MHz. "Not likely," I volunteered. "We're 600 miles from Addis Ababa and well off any airways." Even so, I cranked up my KX 99 and put out a mayday.

To my astonishment, I got an immediate answer from a formal British voice. "Aircraft in distress, this is Gulf Air 342. May we be of assistance?"

The Gulf Air pilot took down our names, aircraft registration, home phone numbers, and position and agreed to relay our details by HF to Addis Ababa. He also promised to call our wives when he landed in Sudan and let them know we were down but not out.

Question was, what now? We had 3 gallons of water, a few days of food, four space blankets, two ELTs, an emergency axe, a new Apple computer and, oh yeah, four life vests and a raft. Just what we needed.

If you wanted to be dead in a place such as this, the possibilities were endless. We'd avoided the reaper in the crash, however, so we counted ourselves one step ahead.

Traditional wisdom suggested we should remain with the aircraft, but I had my doubts. I knew Ethiopia had essentially no search-and-rescue assets, so it was unlikely they'd be coming to get us except perhaps in a truck. What passed for the game trail we'd landed on appeared to point the way to Mandera, Kenya, 60 air miles distant, but what chance would we have of making it in 114-degree heat?

We were on the ground for only about three hours when, to our amazement, a huge, three-axle Mercedes truck came lumbering down the road at all of 5 mph and stopped by the airplane. The young Somali driver spoke a few words of English, and Thomas, a Canadian resident of Nairobi, spoke a few words of various African languages. Between the two of them, we managed to arrange for a ride to the nearest village. It was 50 torturous miles and took almost eight hours, with six stops to let locals jump on or off the truck.

It seemed everyone along the road had a gun of some kind, everything from Russian AK-47s to antique British Enfield rifles or American Colt .45 semi-automatic pistols. I had a Swiss Army knife. I learned later that Somali raiders often crossed into Ethiopia looking for food or whatever else they could steal. You have to be pretty hard up to steal from an Ethiopian.

Our destination village turned out to be Dolo, Ethiopia, 6 miles from the Somali border. There was no power and no phone, but there was a Save The Children compound, funded by the U.S. The manager spoke excellent English and took good care of us. He had a generator and an HF radio, and contacted Addis Ababa, requesting instructions.

We spent four days in beautiful, scenic Dolo, behind a wall of thorn bushes, eating mangos and drinking orangeade. On the fifth morning, a talented Ethiopian pilot landed the world's rattiest-looking Cessna 404 Titan on an impossibly short section of incredibly rough, narrow, dirt road. Despite my absolute certainty that we really were about to die this time, we loaded up, and that pilot somehow managed to coax the big Titan back off the dirt without running into a grass hut.

Two days later in Addis Ababa, the Ethiopian CAA held an informal hearing, determined that we'd apparently done nothing wrong and broken no laws, and we were free to go.

I was surprised to learn a few weeks later that Thomas Jones went back to Ethiopia, salvaged the airplane, loaded it into a pallet in Djibouti, shipped it back to Santa Monica and had it rebuilt. I test flew the totally repaired airplane six months later. Thomas rode quietly in the right seat for a few minutes, then handed me the keys when we got back on the ground and said, "Sell it."

I did exactly that, and there's an owner in Memphis who now owns one of the world's nicest, and most traveled, Piper Lances — or at least, he did last time I checked.

A Cessna rests in the Serengeti.

Part 3: Ferrying a Caravan

It's only 6:30 a.m. and I'm already sweating as I climb the ladder to the new Caravan's cockpit. It's November, but here in Libreville, Gabon, the equator knows no season but summer. The sun steams up above the dense jungle to the east, low and fat against the horizon, and I'm eager to ascend into cooler air.

I'm ready to leave the ground for other reasons, too. Yesterday, as I was refueling the airplane near the short grass at the edge of the ramp, I saw the grass rustling behind the airplane and mentioned it to the young fueler. He looked back, and said, "Oh, don't worry, probably just a cobra." He calmly picked up his machete and walked off into the grass, barefoot and wearing only a pair of shorts. I saw the snake raise its flared hood slightly above the grass, before the boy swung the machete once and stepped back over to the airplane as casually as if he did this sort of thing every day.

While he continued to fuel the Caravan, I took a few tentative steps into the grass in Reeboks and Levi's to find a decapitated cobra still writhing in the grass.

This is my 16th trip to Africa, but just as before, I can't tell anyone along the route of my real destination. Like most other ferry pilots who fly Africa regularly, I carry a second, "conflict" passport with no South African visas in it. A South African stamp would probably cause me to be denied entry to any of the other African countries I must transit.

My final destination is officially listed as Gaborone, Botswana, 140 miles southeast of Johannesburg, again because my flight plan would be denied if I listed my true point of arrival. After every trip, I wonder if officials in the countries I transit are mystified at what must be dozens of new airplanes parked on the ramp in Botswana.

Most of the Caravan's cargo area behind me is taken up by seven 55-gallon drums of jet fuel, adding an extra 2,500 pounds of Jet A to the airplane's standard 2,200-pound capacity. That's over 700 gallons total for somewhere between 16 and 18 hours of endurance. On this trip, "my" Caravan flies at a fat gross of nearly 10,000 pounds, about 1,300 over the normal weight limit.

Today, I should need only about 10 hours to fly the 1,500 nm down the west coast of Africa to Windhoek, Namibia. In theory, I'll arrive in Windhoek with nearly enough fuel to go on to Johannesburg.

The good news about ferrying a Caravan is that it's a great ride. The airplanes are usually well-equipped, extremely roomy and comfortable, and very stable instrument platforms. The bad news is that Caravans are slow — typically 145 knots with the heavy fuel load. Accordingly, we fly early to utilize daylight for the long legs.

As this day begins and the sun climbs well above the horizon, I start the PT-6, call the tower, verify that the runway lights are definitely off (otherwise, I would be charged light fees — day or night) and taxi to the holding point. African airports always seem to find innovative ways to extract fees from pilots, and though this trip is on a pilot fee plus expenses, I try to avoid all the fees I can.

Despite the heavy load, the Caravan levitates off the ground like an elevator and starts uphill at an easy 800 fpm. I climb away from the psychedelic green jungle toward the building cumulus that resides 24/7 along the intertropical convergence zone or ITCZ (inevitably slandarized by pilots as the ITCH). It's not uncommon for cumulonimbus activity to last for several days and nights on the ITCH, but last night was clear, and today the muscular cumulus are slow in building.

Finally level at 11,000 feet, I'm well on top of the clouds, cruising at 160 knots with the help of slight tailwinds. South of the equator now, the clouds begin to slope downhill as I cross over Tchibanga VOR at the bottom of Gabon and turn 45 degrees right to angle offshore. South of Gabon, Congo and Angola are not especially friendly to overflying American aircraft, so most ferry pilots sidestep 20-30 miles off the west African coast to be well out of rifle and TOW missile range, then track south paralleling the 11-degree east meridian, watching Angola pass safely by far to the left.

In the early '80s, two ferry pilots, Jeff Tyler and Tom Willett, served prison terms in Luanda for the crime of having engine problems and landing in Angola without permission. I have resolved to go into the water before I'll land on the beach in Angola.

I make my obligatory transmissions on HF as if I expect a response, and on some trips, I actually receive one or two. Position reports are something of an exercise in futility in this part of the world, anyway. If you do go down, you'd best bring a compass and a paddle so you can find land on your own.

I drift south over the water, more comfortable than over land when that land is Africa. Far off in the distance, I can barely make out infamous Luanda, the best reason I can think of to avoid this part of the continent.

As I track south toward Namibia, the land transitions from double canopy rain forest to arid desert, one of the driest in the world. The Namib Desert begins in southern Angola and runs 400 miles along the coast through Namibia and on down to Capetown, South Africa. It receives only about a half-inch of rainfall a year. And you thought the Sahara was dry.

Eight hours out, I see the white hook of Tiger Island protruding out into the ocean, formerly a peninsula shaped by the outflow of the Cunene River, the border between Angola and Namibia. I turn left toward the distant coast, knowing it's now safe to overfly the land. I pass barren Brandberg Mountain and descend into Windhoek's Eros Airport two minutes ahead of schedule.

The following day, I climb the Caravan's ladder for the last time and head out across the Kalahari Desert toward Johannesburg. Like the Namib, the Kalahari redefines "dry," but much of it is interlaced with dirt roads, so at least you'll have company if you go down. The area is dotted with dry lakes, known as "pans" in this part of the world, all flat — nearly ideal emergency landing sites.

I overfly Gaborone, angle southeast toward Joburg, and finally land at Rand Airport four hours after leaving Windhoek.

As I hand the airplane's logbooks and keys to the new owner, I'm told that this Caravan will be configured with 12 seats and go into immediate service flying tourists into a game park in the Okavango Swamp area of Northern Botswana. I also learn that I'm wanted in Vero Beach, Florida, ASAP to pick up the first production Piper Mirage for delivery to Kassel, Germany.

No rest for the stupid — err, make that wicked — I guess.

The cliffs of Funchal near Madeira, Portugal, make for some challenging flight.

Part 4: Double Engine Failure

You might call the approach to the runway at Funchal, Madeira Islands, Portugal, challenging, especially if you're flying on an even modestly windy day.

In my case, I went into Funchal in a typical wind event, flying a new Cessna T303 Crusader, a medium twin intended to compete head-to-head with Piper's wildly successful Seneca.

It was December 1981, and "my" Cessna T303 was the first Crusader to be ferried overseas. My destination was Johannesburg, South Africa, roughly halfway around the world.

Under contract to Globe Aero of Lakeland, Florida, I'd picked up the airplane at the Cessna factory in Wichita and hurried down to Lakeland for tanking.

Two days later, I flew the Crusader to Bangor, Maine, then on to St. Johns, Newfoundland, the following day.

The next leg was a 1,900 nm overwater hop, diagonally across the Atlantic to the aforementioned Funchal, 700 nm off the south coast of Morocco. I'd never been into that particular airport, but its reputation preceded it. The consensus was, it could get exciting when the wind was woofing, and the wind at Funchal was nearly always woofing.

The Madeira Islands, famous for Madeira wine, are mostly rugged hills and low mountains, so there was little room for a conventional runway at Funchal. Accordingly, the airport was built at the apex of a half-moon bay; the approach is semi-circular practically all the way to touchdown. Navy pilots should love it.

The threshold is constructed on pylons that begin 1,000 feet out in the bay and stand 250 feet above the water. The threshold starts you on a fairly steep uphill rollout. Just past the terminal at midfield, the runway begins to level, then turns downhill, so you'd better be pretty well stopped by midfield.

The asphalt extends for more than 5,400 feet — runway length isn't a big problem — but the curving approach to avoid the hills means you're often battling turbulent winds off the mountains all the way to touchdown.

Funchal is on practically everyone's list of the 10 worst airports in the world. The History Channel program "Most Extreme Airports" labeled Funchal the ninth-most dangerous airport in the world and the third-most dangerous in Europe.

There's almost no ramp space at Funchal, so unless you arrive late and depart early the next morning, you can only fuel up, grab a sandwich, and leave town.

I arrived late with two other ferry aircraft, a Mooney 231, and a Piper Seneca. All three of us were headed for Rand Airport in Johannesburg. Technical problems with further clearances held us up for an extra day, so we had an additional 24 hours to prepare for Africa.

The bad news was that the only refueling truck with avgas wasn't a truck at all. It was a trailer with no power to drive the pump. This meant the poor kid selling fuel had to cycle a manual swing arm pump to fill our tanks for the next leg across the Sahara to Abidjan, Ivory Coast (officially the Republic of Côte d'Ivoire). The young gas boy must have cycled that pump a thousand times to fill our three airplanes.

Even worse, I was the last airplane to be refueled, and the trailer ran dry before the Crusader's last ferry tank was full. This meant whatever miscellaneous glorp that might have accumulated at the bottom of the trailer's tank may have gone straight into my ferry tanks. Fortunately, all other tanks were already topped.

Sadly, there are no convenient quick drains at the bottom of ferry tanks. Owners aren't enthusiastic about ferry companies cutting holes into the belly of their new airplane to install them. That meant the only way I could check the ferry fuel for contamination was to climb on top of the tank, unscrew the cap and shine a flashlight inside. Not much chance of seeing anything deep down in the bottom of the tanks.

We departed Funchal the following morning and headed southeast toward Mauritania and the Sahara. The day's destination was Abidjan, Ivory Coast, known to be in a near-constant state of revolution.

Funchal Airport

As we tracked above a desert roughly the size of the contiguous United States, I watched the two fuel flow needles fluttering slightly on the single gauge. The engines were running smooth and all other indications were normal, so I wrote it off as an instrument problem.

We passed Bamako, Mali, about 200 nm from the infamous city of legend, Timbuktu; then, Yamoussoukro (capitol of Ivory Coast), and continued to Abidjan with no mechanical complaints. The fuel flows were still flittering slightly as I turned final for Abidjan. Just the gauge, I reminded myself.

Safely on the ground, I talked to the Seneca pilot, Ernie Kuney, an A&P mechanic, and he dismissed the problem as a typical new-airplane glitch.

Like so much of Arica in those days, Ivory Coast was in a perpetual state of revolution. It seemed there were soldiers with AK-47s everywhere we went, including the parking lot and lobby of the Intercontinental Hotel. For a pilot making his first trip to a developing nation, the constant presence of military personnel and vehicles was unnerving.

The following day's flight would be a short one, only about 850 nm across the Gulf of Guinea to Libreville, Gabon. Again, I watched the fuel flows ticking occasionally as our three airplanes flew over water toward out next-to-last stop. Everything else seemed normal.

We arrived early enough for me to catch the mechanic at Cessna of Gabon. He'd never even seen a photo of a Crusader before (hardly anyone else had, either), but he reassured me that it was "most certainly the gauge." Most certainly hope so.

The next day's leg was 1,500 nm down the west coast of Africa to Windhoek, Namibia. The other two pilots had flown this route before, and they suggested turning slightly right at the Congo River, flying out to sea at least 30 miles to avoid Angolan airspace altogether: then, traveling 1,000 nm straight south until reaching the Tiger Peninsula. Tiger was a small, sandy, white spit of land, outlet of the Cunene River to the South Atlantic and Angola's border with Namibia.

After that, we could turn slightly left, back over the coastal Namib Desert and on into Windhoek without fear of being shot at. Angola and Namibia were at war at the time, and Angola had virtually no air force. Accordingly, they assumed any airplane was an enemy machine. This provided a strong incentive to stay out over the Atlantic until we were well clear of Angola.

I'd been warned that there were few radio navaids in this part of the world, and most of the ones that did exist were inop. Sure enough, the trip so far had demonstrated that only about one in five was working.

For that reason, navigation in much of Africa was mostly point-and-shoot or flying by landmarks. This was long before the introduction of GPS, so finding a destination was relegated to whatever worked.

Twitchy fuel flows again. The gauge — right?

To everyone's surprise, there was a VOR near the equator in southern Gabon with a strong signal and a name right out of a Tarzan movie, Tchibanga (TCH, if memory serves). As we passed over it level at 11,000 feet and made our turn off the coast, I pushed my seat all the way back, repositioned the right seat forward so I could put my feet up and let the Crusader's autopilot do the work.

Directly below, I could see the almost iridescent green, double-canopy rain forest stretching in every direction except west, a near solid blanket of thick jungle with few open spaces. Wouldn't want to go down in this part of Africa.

I'd reluctantly switched to the aft, 100-gallon ferry tank a few minutes before, the one that was last to be fueled in Funchal. We always departed and landed on the wing tanks, usually the farthest forward. Ferry tanks were nearly always installed in the back of the airplane.

There was the predictable pause of disbelief, during which the autopilot disconnected and the left wing dropped toward the jungle. The right engine also quit before I could even react, and the Crusader's nose pitched down toward the impenetrable tangle of trees below.

For that reason, we had to switch to the farthest aft tank as soon as possible to keep the CG from shifting too far aft. I watched the fuel flows to make certain there was no change; nothing too erratic.

By now, I was convinced I was just being paranoid and that everyone else was right. The fuel flow problem seemed to be more imagination than real.

I opened a package of chocolate chip cookies, popped the top off a bottle of water and settled down for the long ride south.

That's when the left engine quit.

There was the predictable pause of disbelief, during which the autopilot disconnected and the left wing dropped toward the jungle. The right engine also quit before I could even react, and the Crusader's nose pitched down toward the impenetrable tangle of trees below.

I hit the pumps, switched back to the wing tanks, pushed the mixtures forward, eased them back, and generally tried to undo anything I might have done wrong in the last minute or two. Nothing helped.

Each of the two 100-gallon ferry tanks fed both engines at the same time, a concession to simplicity. That meant the same tank was fueling, or in this case, defueling, both engines simultaneously. Whatever was blocking fuel flow to the engines had probably come out of the aft ferry tank and switching back to the mains had not solved the problem.

I squeaked out a mayday to my two playmates. "Tom and Ernie, I just lost power on both engines."

Ernie came back first, "Bill, don't screw around on the radio."

Tom Willett jumped in next, apparently recognizing that I didn't normally talk with that high a voice. "Bill, where are you?"

"Tom, I'm right behind you, have you in sight. I'm about a mile back, circling to the left," I replied, desperately searching for an opening in the trees below. The only flat spot I could see was a small, lazy river flowing toward the coast. I'd rather take my chances with crocodiles than try to dodge the trees.

After 8,000 hours of accident-free flying, it was beginning to look as if I was about to wreck my first airplane. Even worse, I might even wreck me.

No more ferry flights. I'll never see space. What about the girl back home? Who'll feed my dogs?

After 8,000 hours of accident-free flying, it was beginning to look as if I was about to wreck my first airplane. Even worse, I might even wreck me.

"I'm coming back," said Tom, interrupting my cynical reverie. "There's a small, grass, missionary strip around here somewhere. I saw it on my last trip."

Both engines were staggering, chugging out occasional short bursts of power, then reverting to idle. Neither engine had quit completely, but that was little consolation.

Before I'd left Wichita 10 days before, I'd asked one of the Crusader test pilots what speed he'd suggest for best glide at 15% to 20% over gross. He chuckled and replied, "Tell you what. If you need to use that speed on your trip, let us know what it is when you get back." Neither Cessna nor any other manufacturer I know of does flight testing at such high gross weights.

I pegged the airspeed at 110 knots and tried not to look at the VSI as I augured down in the general direction of the river.

The radio came alive with an announcement by Tom Willett in the Mooney. "Bill, I have you in sight, and I've spotted the grass strip," he said. "It's just north of you."

I rolled out of the turn to the north but didn't see anything even vaguely resembling a flat spot between the trees, much less a grass runway. The Crusader was gliding like a Steinway, and when I finally picked up the strip, I was practically overhead, the wrong place to try to improvise a pattern without power.

I couldn't begin to guess how long the runway was, but it looked far too short for a 6,000-pound twin. I widened out to the east in a modified semblance of an abbreviated downwind leg, turned base and hurried the airplane around to final. As I rolled out, I dropped the wheels and flaps, only to realize I'd already blown it. I was going to be short. "Expletive deleted."

I was glad the airplane had no cockpit voice recorder, as I braced for impact. I was about to crash the first Crusader to leave the U.S.

The airplane cleared the trees by inches and slammed down well short of the runway, splattering mud everywhere. It half-skidded/half-bounced out of the tall grass onto the short strip. To my utter amazement, nothing had punched up through the top wing skins, despite the hard impact. Somehow, the T303's rugged trailing beam gear system had protected me from evil.

The Cessna rolled out a short distance, and I turned off to the left with the last of my momentum as Tom Willett buzzed me in the Mooney. He gave me a congratulatory wing waggle, then pulled up, entered an abbreviated pattern, and landed.

Ernie was still circling above at 11,000 feet in the Seneca, and he was talking to Air Gabon in Libreville on VHF. Tom advised him that my airplane appeared undamaged, and I was still breathing and had no pieces missing. Ernie relayed the news to Air Gabon. They immediately launched a rescue Skylane with a mechanic and tools aboard.

We pulled the top cowls, and just as I'd suspected, both engines had ingested foreign material, presumably from the aft ferry tank. It appeared to be a half-dissolved fabric substance, and it had plugged up fuel flow to both engines. We never understood why it took so long to shut down fuel flow.

We saved as much of the contaminant as possible in a plastic baggie, and I sent it to Shell for analysis after I got home. Their report suggested it was a long-outdated, fabric filter that was no longer used but was supposed to be changed every six months when in service. They estimated this material was at least three years old.

We pulled the top cowls, and just as I'd suspected, both engines had ingested foreign material, presumably from the aft ferry tank. It appeared to be a half-dissolved fabric substance, and it had plugged up fuel flow to both engines.

The mechanic did the best he could to clean out the injector lines and filters; then, wished me luck for the short flight back to Libreville. Willet and I drained as much fuel as we could from both ferry tanks to reduce the load for takeoff.

I staggered out of Tchibanga with nearly full wing tanks and managed to sneak back into Libreville barely before the nighttime curfew.

The following day, there were 20 cars lined up outside the Air Gabon maintenance hangar. All the owners were eager to collect their allotment of 10 gallons each, as the Crusader's entire fuel system was drained of every ounce of 100 octane, probably close to 200 gallons. Each driver strained his 10 gallons through a chamois before pouring it into his car's gas tank.

Willett's Mooney had been fueled just before mine in Funchal, so Air Gabon checked his fuel and found the same fibrous contaminants. As a result, his airplane's fuel and injection system also had to be drained and cleaned — another free 130 gallons for the Gabon Auto Club.

The remainder of the trip was anti-climactic. Willett and I launched out of Libreville for Namibia on December 29, spent the 30th cleaning up the airplanes in Windhoek, and finally made the last leg across the Kalahari Desert to Johannesburg on December 31.

Cessna's South African dealer held a big New Year's party in honor of the first Crusader's safe arrival. It seemed everyone had heard about the double engine failure and subsequent emergency landing in Gabon.

I told the story a dozen or more times, and I was an instant curiosity for about 10 of my allotted 15 minutes of fame.

13

The Great Barrier Reef turns into the beautiful
region of Cairns in northeast Australia.

Flying Over Down Under

Imagine a 2,200-mile-wide desert island with magnificent cities built on the coasts. That's Australia.

Flying down from Guadalcanal in the Solomon Islands, your course line slowly merges with Australia's east coast as you sneak in from the left. The angle is so slight, you may not even notice the land of Oz until you're practically feet dry.

The country seems to simply materialize in the stark beauty of the Coral Sea. If your destination is Brisbane and the weather is severe clear, you can spot the coast from two hours out, as the ocean below becomes shallower and begins to justify its name as the Great Barrier Reef.

NASA tells us the reef is the Earth's largest living feature that may be seen from space, and you begin to understand the enormity of the reef as you look down at the menagerie of color below. The 1,200-nm reef runs along most of the country's east coast, a scuba diver's paradise if you ignore the occasional shark or sea snake.

On my first trip Down Under (do Aussies call the rest of the world "Up Over"?) in 1992, I made landfall at Cairns, far up on the northeast corner of the island continent, a lush, tropical paradise a mere 17 degrees south from the equator, about the same distance south as San Juan, Puerto Rico, is north.

Cairns is one of Australia's most beautiful cities, fronted by the western Pacific and backed by the Great Dividing Range of mountains. For much of the year, Cairns luxuriates in warm weather and sunshine, with occasional light rain and puffy cumulus clouds.

I was flying a Cessna Skymaster on that first 7,500-nm trip, and after a comfortable overnight in downtown Cairns, I fired up early the next morning and prepared to launch for my final destination of Perth, flying diagonally across the country. It would be hard to find two locations in Australia more distant than Cairns and Perth.

When the controller asked my destination on my "no details" flight plan, and I told him Perth, there was a short pause ... then, "What stops are you planning for fuel?"

"None," I said.

Another longer pause, then, "Sir, are you aware of the distance from Cairns to Perth?"

"Yes sir," I replied. "The Garmin says 1,860 nautical miles."

He keyed the mic once more, and I heard conversation in the background. Short pause, then, "Oh yes, you're the American ferry flight that came in from the Solomons last night. OK, you're cleared to taxi to the holding point for runway ..."

Once in the air, I urged the Skymaster just high enough to clear the Great Dividing Range and pointed the nose southwest toward Alice Springs and Uluru, better known as Ayers Rock, close to the geographic center of the country. After I'd passed the coastal mountains, I descended to roughly 500 feet above the terrain and settled in for the 14-hour flight.

The vast majority of Australia's population lives on the coasts of the country in major cities such as Canberra, Cairns, Townsville, Brisbane, Sydney, Melbourne, Adelaide, Perth, and Darwin. As mentioned above, the only significant city in the interior is Alice Springs, population 26,500, isolated from the coasts by 500-1,000 nm of desert in all directions.

As the miles slid by, little changed below the airplane. The Australian Outback could easily pass for the American Southwest except for the lack of mountains and the dominance of termite mounds, thousands of them. Occasionally, I noticed the tan/brown earth interrupted by surges of life, kangaroos flowing across the outback, bouncing sporadically in every direction. There was little to slow them down.

Nature abhors straight lines and symmetry, and you won't find much of either in the outback. There are few roads — paved, dirt or any other kind — minimum power lines, and only sporadic railroad tracks.

Even more significant, there are few fences, a standard signpost to even lightly populated spaces. In much of the rest of the world, fences are a giveaway to the presence of man. Roads, power lines, railroad tracks, and fences often follow straight lines, and in much of the outback, there's simply no need for straight lines. You can fly for a half hour or more without spotting even the slightest manifestation of humans.

Uluru, aka Ayers Rock.

The "stations" (ranches in U.S. speak) are huge by comparison to their American counterparts. The outback is so arid, it requires large expanses of grazing land to feed cattle or sheep. Here in the U.S., the largest ranch covers just under a million acres. In Australia, million-acre stations are common, and the biggest of all covers nearly 6 million acres, which is roughly the size of Maryland.

With such enormous areas to patrol, many owners of stations police them by aircraft, either fixed wing or helicopter. Don't plan on seeing many in the interior of Australia, however. The country is so large, it swallows up literally thousands of stations of all shapes and sizes. Owners of these gigantic properties rarely patrol them.

One of the great attractions of Australia is Ayers Rock, 210 nm southwest of Alice Springs. I pulled up to 3,000 feet crossing Alice Springs, then veered slightly left to head for Uluru, the Aborigine name for the huge attraction. The large sandstone rock formation stands alone, about 1,000 feet tall, and if you think there couldn't possibly be any air traffic here in the middle of Australia, you'd think wrong.

Texas Wheel in the Outback at Tumut New South Wales Australia.

I set up a left orbit of the rock formation about 1,000 feet above the crest, only to spot a 737 coming the other way around 1,000 feet above me. At the time, there was airline service from Sydney or Melbourne that provided flightseeing tours of Uluru. I turned away to let the big guy cruise by in a 20-degree bank. When he finished his first circle, he reversed direction and flew a tight 360 in the opposite path, presumably to allow passengers on both sides of the airplane to see and photograph this famous Australian landmark.

With my flight almost half over, I turned back on course and continued southwest toward Perth, another 1,100 nm. West of Alice Springs, Australia becomes a haven for mining, especially gold mining. In fact, the Skymaster's owner, Blair Howe, had been a hard rock miner for 30 years until the day he swung his pick for the millionth time, and there it was. Howe had finally hit a major vein of gold and struck it rich.

He sold his claim to a major mining company and went into the business of transporting people and equipment around the Great Sandy Desert near Mt. Magnet in Western Australia.

When I finally handed him the Skymaster's keys the following day, I asked about the problem of prop strikes on the rear propeller from rocks and debris kicked up by the front prop and main gear. (The Skymaster mounts its two engines on the front and rear of the cabin rather than on the wings). Cessna had anticipated the possibility of over-rotation on unimproved runways and had mounted the rear engine with a thrust line 6 inches higher than that of the front engine. I still wondered about damage to the rear prop during operation on rocky or dirt strips.

Blair smiled and opened the door to a storage shed directly behind the airplane's parking spot, and there stood four shiny new propellers wrapped in plastic, waiting for service. Blair's pilot and I compared notes the following morning over breakfast before flying down to Perth for my Qantas commute to Sydney and on to Los Angeles the following day.

Even though virtually everything worth seeing in Australia is on the coasts of the country, it's a beautiful destination if you have an airplane with a range of, oh, maybe 2,500 nm or so.

14

Nauru – A Tropical Disaster

This small island nation hosted an unusual, unforgettable trip.

I wondered why on Earth (or more accurately, water) anyone would want to live there. As it turns out, hardly anyone does.

I've overflown Nauru perhaps a dozen times. It's almost directly online between Majuro, Marshall Islands (smack in the geographic center of the Pacific) and famous Henderson Field at Honiara, Solomon Islands.

When I was delivering airplanes to Australia regularly in the '80s and '90s, I often looked down on the small, oval-shaped island 26 miles south of the equator. Its interior is now moonscaped and jagged, looking like something out of a science fiction movie. I wondered why on Earth (or more accurately, water) anyone would want to live there.

As it turns out, hardly anyone does. Nauru is a relatively tiny dot in the Pacific, only 8 miles across, and because of its proximity to the equator, it's subject to the vagaries of weather peculiar to the sometimes-unpredictable intertropical convergence zone. It's the world's smallest island nation featuring a population of only 9,000, one airport, a single 12-mile coastal highway, and, until recently, an economy totally dependent upon, well, bird droppings.

Technically, the mining product is called phosphate, and it's used all over the world in the production of fertilizer. Nice to be known for something, I guess.

At one time, phosphate mining provided natives of Nauru with the Pacific's highest per capita income, along with the world's highest obesity rate, over 90 percent. More than coincidentally, Nauru also suffers from the highest type 2 diabetes rate, with 40% of the population affected.

For years, when phosphate mining was proceeding apace, the otherwise inconspicuous island was known as the "Kuwait of the South Pacific." There was no income tax, most government services were free, and virtually everyone was rich, all thanks to those obliging sea birds.

Trouble was, phosphate was the island country's *only* resource. Nauru had practically nothing else to offer. The beaches weren't anything special, so tourism was unlikely, there wasn't much vegetation and there was limited fresh water provided by an aging desalination plant that broke down on alternate Thursdays. In short, there was little reason to visit Nauru unless you were in the guano business.

Mining experts had long warned the Nauru government that the supply of phosphate was dangerously finite and it would run out quickly if the country didn't manage it properly. Nauru's succession of administrations ignored the advice and continued to plunder the interior of the island, gradually stripping away all vegetation and eventually leaving an uninhabitable, volcano-like surface over 80% of the country's 12 square miles.

A combination of corruption, government malfeasance, and bad business decisions caused the phosphate to be essentially depleted by the beginning of this century. Today, Nauru is an economic and environmental disaster area. Unemployment is around 23% and 95% of working residents are employed by the government.

When the country was riding high, it had the obligatory international airline consisting of a number of Boeing 737s. Gradually, as the phosphate disappeared and the economy scaled back, Air Nauru (now renamed Our Airline) sold off its jets until there was only one remaining. That one was a 737-300 (VH-RON), and it was famous in the South Pacific. In those days, it flew all over the region, from Hong Kong, Manila, and Guam to Nadi (Fiji), Brisbane, Pago Pago and Apia (Samoa), and Honiara.

My chance to fly on Air Nauru came in 1997. I had contracted to pick up a Fijian-registered '58 Baron in Tarawa, Kiribati, and return it to California. The airplane had been flying back and forth from the international airport at Nadi, Fiji, to a small strip on the island

Photo courtesy of the U.S. Department of Energy's
Atmospheric Radiation Measurement Program.

of Vanua Levu, a few miles from a resort hotel. The Air Pacific 747
captain who owned both the Baron and the hotel had decided the
job could be done just as well and a lot cheaper by a Twin Otter
commuter that serviced the islands.

Accordingly, I flew an Air Pacific jumbo to Nadi, stayed an extra
three days to pick up a Fijian pilot's license (hey, it's a tough job)
and finally boarded one of Air Nauru's twice-a-week flights to Tarawa where the Baron was allegedly ready to go.

The Air Nauru Boeing was overbooked, but the captain, a friendly Australian, volunteered the empty jump seat in the cockpit. (This
was obviously pre-9/11.)

The Boeing looked brand new. It was immaculate inside and
out, though the panel betrayed it as an older generation FLUF (ask
an airline pilot). As it turned out, the sole remaining Air Nauru

airplane was totally crewed and maintained by Qantas out of Melbourne, Australia.

It was the co-pilot's leg to fly, and the captain and I commiserated about common friends and destinations around the South Pacific, and airplanes in general. As we drifted northwest toward Tarawa, looking down from 35,000 feet on myriad ring atolls, dazzling coral reefs and bottomless blue ocean, I couldn't help reflecting on the differences between my kind of flying and airline travel.

The Boeing sailed smoothly along with rock solid stability, cruising at 460 knots far above the occasional weather, compared to my normal 170-200 knots in the airspace below 18,000 feet where the turbulence gods hold their parties.

We tracked on toward the Kiribati Islands, and the captain told me a little about flying for Air Nauru. He'd been flying under contract for a few years, and he loved it.

He said it was great to only have to fly one airplane, so he knew that particular 737 extremely well. The Boeing was easy to handle and had good short-field characteristics, an important advantage on some abbreviated Pacific island strips. The legs were mostly short, and Pacific weather was generally benign, except for the occasional typhoon. The route structure had contracted considerably since Nauru's glory days, and he knew most of the approaches by heart, all factors that made the flying comfortable and fun.

Perhaps the most amazing detail about Air Nauru was that the single Boeing was flying an average of 100 hours a *week*. In fact, it was more like 100 hours in six days, as most of the seventh day was dedicated to maintenance and a 100-hour inspection, usually conducted in Melbourne. (The latter inspection is a requirement for ICAO signatory countries.)

That meant the 737 was being operated about 17 hours a day (obviously with multiple crews), six days a week. It took seven dedicated, two-man crews to keep the airplane in the air for a full 5,300 hours a year. Now, *that's* impressive utilization. I put 110 hours on my Mooney last year.

The Baron turned out to be a dud. The ferry tanks didn't work and the HF radio was deaf and dumb, so I wound up flying back to Nadi the following day and home to California while the folks at Tarawa got things sorted out. I returned two weeks later and flew Air Nauru one last time from Nadi to Tarawa, as luck would have it with the same crew.

As the lightly loaded Boeing leaped out of Tarawa and headed back to Pago Pago, I couldn't help envying the crew's first-class ride across the Pacific. I'd need at least 15 hours the following day to make Honolulu, and by that time, they'd probably be home in Australia or relaxing by the pool at the Rainmaker Hotel in Pago Pago.

The path not taken.

The Secrets of Johnston Island

How much reserve is enough when crossing the Pacific?

Majuro in the Marshall Islands has to be one of the world's more remote locations. It's smack in the middle of the Pacific, 1,600 miles east of Guam and 2,000 miles southwest of Hawaii.

Until a few years ago when Mobil stopped refining avgas, Majuro was a standard stop for piston aircraft on the road to Australia, Japan, and points throughout Indonesia. I made perhaps two dozen trips through the Marshalls in the 1990s, flying mostly new Mooneys, Cessna 206s, and Piper Mirages to or from Australia and Japan. In case you've never heard of the Marshalls, think Bikini Atoll. Does that clarify it?

On one 11,000-nm ferry flight eastbound from Sendai, Japan, to Aachen, Germany (the wrong way around), in 1999, I was flying a near-new Mirage with a neoprene-bladder ferry tank in back. This was my first (and thankfully only) trip with a bladder tank, and I was eager to be done with it. Read on.

After a relatively uneventful crossing from Sendai down to Guam, and a similarly simple transition over Majuro, I departed the Marshall Islands at 6:30 a.m. and climbed out in the direction of Johnston Island, the next landfall almost 1,300 miles distant and directly on line to Honolulu. Predictable trade winds were in my face all the way, subtracting perhaps 15-20 knots from the airplane's 200-knot true airspeed at FL210. The Pacific was benign on that smooth, clear morning in May as I tracked backwards in time toward yesterday and Honolulu, 20 degrees on the "front" side of the international date line.

Just over seven hours out, Johnston came into view far ahead, partially hidden beneath scattered popcorn cumulus beginning to materialize as the day heated up. If the bad news about the Pacific is that there's often nothing to see but millions of square miles of ocean, the good news is that the visibility is excellent.

The Mirage was flying smooth and happy, and so was I as we tracked on toward Honolulu at 180 knots. The flight plan suggested the leg would be only about 11.5 hours, a relatively short hop before a day off in Honolulu.

The faint odor of avgas is nearly constant in tanked ferry airplanes, but as I closed on Johnston, the fuel odor became stronger. Within a few minutes, it was obvious I had a leak in the ferry tank, and the odor was becoming overpowering.

I advised San Francisco long range of my problem on HF, then immediately initiated an emergency descent. Level at 10,000 feet, I dumped the cabin pressurization, popped open the left storm window, and leaned forward to breathe the clean Pacific air. Johnston was only 30 miles away now, a small, rectangular island partially covered by a 9,000-foot runway, hangars, and a clutch of suspicious Quonset huts cluttering what was left of its surface.

Johnston was the worst-kept secret in the Pacific. During the '60s, it had been headquarters for the nuclear weapons atmospheric tests. Now, practically everyone knew it was America's repository for chemical and biological weapons. The U.S. Air Force was systematically burning them up in furnaces at the southwest corner of the island. The trades blow so consistently across Johnston from Hawaii that the smoke plume nearly always blows straight toward the Marshalls, 1,300 nm away with not even a rock in between. The thinking was that if there were ever an accidental release of chemical or biological agents, it would have plenty of time and distance to dissipate. (Still, traditional wisdom in the general aviation ferry business was never to cross Johnston below 10,000 feet. "Doctor, I have this strange cough ... ")

For obvious reasons, landing at Johnston was strictly prohibited unless you had a real emergency. Running short of fuel was not considered "real." A Beech A55 Baron on the same route had gone in there two weeks before when his how-goes-it suggested he'd misjudged the winds and wouldn't make Kauai, and the Air Force had not been sympathetic. With not a drop of avgas on the island, they'd put the pilot on the first military shuttle back to Honolulu where he had to arrange for shipment of two barrels of fuel to Johnston, return, refuel the airplane, and continue the trip. Subtract $5,000 from any profit.

I dialed up Johnston's frequency and punched the push-to-talk. "Johnston, November 3274B, we're 30 southwest out of Majuro on an IFR for Honolulu, and it looks as if we have a fuel leak in a ferry tank."

Short pause, then, "Roger 74B, this is Johnston, how may we be of service?"

He doesn't get it, I thought. "Johnston, I don't know how long I've been leaking or how much fuel I've lost. The fuel odor is pretty overpowering," I said.

Long pause, then, "Sir, you have to say the words," came the bored reply.

Finally, I relented. "OK, Johnston, November 3274B is declaring a fuel emergency."

"Roger that, 74B. Altimeter is 30.01, wind is 030 at 12 and active runway is 05. Would you like the equipment?" Still bored.

"Negative on the equipment, Johnston," I said. "I'm OK so far. I'll enter a left downwind for 05."

"I understand, 74B. By the way, we'd suggest you not fly through the plume of smoke coming off the smokestacks at the southwest corner of the island." Hmmm.

I overflew the island, entered a downwind, turned tight to avoid the ominous smoke, landed, and taxied into the small terminal building where a jeep full of MPs was waiting — with weapons. They were friendly enough but also very businesslike. While a young lieutenant was checking my paperwork, one airman climbed into the Mirage, rummaged around inside for a few minutes, then came out almost staggering as he climbed down the bottom clamshell.

"Jeez, he's right sir, he has a bad fuel leak. There's nothing in the airplane," the airman told his lieutenant, shaking his head from the fumes. We could see a constant trickle of fuel leaking from the Mirage's belly.

The officer smiled, handed back my license and medical and said, "OK, sir, it appears you had a legitimate emergency, but you need to fix it and leave. This is a top-secret military installation and we have no facilities for civilians here."

While the military cops looked on, I went back to the airplane and discovered the source of the leak in about 30 seconds; a cracked, clear plastic fuel line coming out from the bottom of the rubber tank. Fortunately, there was plenty of extra tubing, so I pulled out my trusty Swiss Army knife, sliced a new length, clamped it in place, and was ready to continue in about five minutes.

Trouble was, now what? How much fuel had I lost? The 150-gallon rubber tank gave me no clue. How much less bulbous should it be when there are five gallons missing? Twenty gallons? How about 30? Fully inflated, the tank is a giant black bubble. How do you measure fuel use when there's no gauge?

Johnston Atoll Photo by Staff Sgt. Val Gempis, USAF/Wikimedia Commons

The leak seemed so small, I couldn't imagine I'd lost much fuel, but I had no way of knowing for sure, and the middle of the Pacific is a bad place for SWAG (scientific wild-assed guess) estimates.

The GPS suggested it was 640 miles to Kauai, 700 to Honolulu. While the Air Force had assured me I wasn't in trouble, they'd made it clear I had to leave now!

I made a SWAG estimate of remaining fuel and then called the tower to have them put me back on file for Honolulu. I climbed back aboard the big Piper and departed Johnston with an uneasy feeling. The plan was to run the fat ferry tank until it was completely flat and empty, then switch back to the main wing tank and finish the trip with some idea of known quantity.

I climbed up to 15,000 feet this time to stay below the worst of the wind and began tracking R584 toward Choko intersection and Honolulu. Before I'd gone far, the depth of my stupidity overwhelmed me. I was crossing the Pacific Ocean, and I didn't know how much fuel I had on board!

I punched the mic button on the HF and told San Francisco I was diverting to Kauai. I turned slightly left, cranked the identifier for Kauai into the GPS, and hoped the wind would be a little friendlier on the new heading. It wasn't. Instead, the Mirage lost about 8 knots as I plunged on into gathering darkness.

As I closed on Kauai, the headwind component increased, and I advised San Francisco to stand by, as I might need help from SAR. I finally saw the lights of the island appear in the distance. By this time, I was back on the 60-gallon main wing tanks, having long since exhausted the rubber ferry tank. My GPS counted down the miles with what seemed glacial speed as both fuel gauges dropped toward zero.

I crossed the southwest coast of Kauai, spotted the rabbit, and followed the lights to the most welcome touchdown I've made anywhere in the world.

Nine gallons. That was the answer to the big question the next day. That's about a half-hour in a Mirage, and if that seems like a lot, remember that I started the day with 270. When we're in our right mind out on the ocean, we like to land with two hours of reserve.

I'll certainly never make that mistake again. But I'll find some new ones.

16

Majuro, Marshall Islands

To Korea, With Luck

Four legs, 52 flight hours in one of the world's most comfortable – and slowest –turboprops.

My buddy Jeff Kopps of the National Weather Service in Monterey had predicted headwinds out of Santa Barbara, and as usual, he was right. It's 2,160 nm to Honolulu, and if I used those initial winds to calculate my how-goes-it, I'd probably never launch, as the numbers suggest I won't make it.

Fortunately, the wind nearly always turns around at mid-crossing, gradually rotating clockwise to the tail for the last 900-1,000 nm. I depart Santa Barbara at 11,400 pounds — 2,700 pounds over gross — and the airplane labors to reach 6,000 feet, which is my initial cruising altitude. Early ground speeds indicate about 130 knots above the Pacific. The airplane wallows along at its heavy weight, struggling to make headway against the wind.

The Cessna Caravan I fly is a capable enough machine, fitted with 410-gallon ferry tanks, bringing total fuel capacity to 745 gallons. That's about 16.6 hours' worth at 45 gph. Still, as a turboprop, it looks as if it should be delivering milk products — wheels down and welded, beefy struts holding the wings in place — a flying cargo hauler doing exactly the job it does best, provided you're not in a hurry.

> *The Cessna Caravan is a capable enough machine. Still, as a turboprop, it looks as if it should be delivering milk products … a flying cargo hauler doing exactly the job it does best, provided you're not in a hurry.*

Under more normal circumstances, I'd be seeing 150 knots at 10,000 feet. Today, to go up is to go slow. I drive on toward Hawaii at the minimum IFR altitude, confident the wind will turn around — it better.

It does. By 1,200 nm out, I have a slight push, and the lighter weight plus the gathering tailwind grant me a 145-knot groundspeed. As I gain on Father Damien's Kalaupapa airport on Molokai, my first point of land in Hawaii, the Caravan's speed slowly increases: 150 knots, 160 knots, 165 knots. Finally, in the last hour of the trip, I'm seeing 170 knots on the Garmin 530. Though I departed Santa Barbara at the first hint of daylight, I land on Honolulu's runway 4R two hours into night, 15.1 hours en route, average speed 142 knots. I have 60 gallons reserve or 1.3 hours remaining in the tanks. The first leg of ferry flight No. 209 is complete.

I spend my day off driving around Oahu in a rental car, marveling at the lack of interstate highways in Hawaii, checking out the Gidget surfing competition at North Shore Beach. Great surfing there. I finally finish the day at Waikiki, still admiring the scenery.

A day later, I'm ready for the second leg of the trip, this one 1,980 nm down to Majuro, Marshall Islands, smack in the middle of the Pacific and just over halfway to my destination. The remote location served its purpose in the '50s when the Marshalls — Kwajalein, Bikini, and Eniwetok — were prime locations for America's atmospheric nuclear weapons tests. Today, the Marshalls are an independent country, though still tied to the USA by treaty, currency, and other agreements. No, the Marshalls don't glow in the dark.

To avoid landing after the 4:45 p.m. curfew in Majuro and incurring an overtime fee, I'm off Honolulu at 6 a.m., well before daybreak. True to Jeff's updated predictions, the winds are the standard prevailing trades, shoving the heavily loaded Caravan along at 150 knots right after level-off at 6,000 feet. Again, higher is not better; it's actually slower. The Cessna is so heavy, I probably couldn't climb to 10,000 feet anyway, at least not until I burn down to a more civilized weight.

Johnston Island comes and goes, 700 miles out, a former U.S. military base, now totally abandoned, its Quonset huts collapsed and hauled away, its runway Xed off. It's another 1,280 nm to Majuro, and there's not even a rock sticking out of the water for refuge.

There is weather ahead, however, ever-present along the intertropical convergence zone (ITCZ), or more simply, the "ITCH." It starts at about 12-15 degrees north latitude with tropical cumulus clouds building well above 10,000 feet. Accordingly, I request FL100 on HF, and San Francisco ARINC approves my climb. No other idiots out

Guam

here today at low altitude. I'm not above the clouds, but at least there's next to no chance of ice, and I'm high enough to more easily circumnavigate the worst of them.

Predictably, the second leg goes quicker. I'm on the ground in Majuro after only 12.3 hours, landing at 4:20 p.m. local tomorrow, 25 minutes ahead of curfew, average speed 161 knots. Like Hawaii and most other Pacific islands, Majuro's runway is built practically right on the water — elevation 6 feet. Rising sea levels from global warming (or whatever the cause) and the threat of tsunami must make the Marshall Islanders nervous.

I fly the next leg to Guam, a mere 1,630 nm due west, punching in and out of rain and scud most of the way, but it's fairly benign weather, nothing to worry about, at least not yet. I drift above a series of tiny islands, most of them characteristic Pacific coral ring atolls, occasionally visible through breaks in the clouds. Again, I start off at 6,000 feet, the minimum IFR altitude to take maximum advantage of the low-level wind, then, drift up to 10,000 when I'm able.

The weather in Guam is rain and yuck, the remnants of Typhoon Nida, and I'm forced to fly the length of the island, make a 180, and shoot the only instrument approach of the trip. The Caravan touches down after only 10.5 hours at 155 knots average speed. In the motorcycle world, these kinds of legs are called Iron Butt. They're much easier to take in a Caravan.

Most of the time, Guam is the Hawaii of Japan, only 1,400 miles southeast of Tokyo, but possessed of a warm, humid climate. Tumon Bay features a dozen high-rise resorts, and they're full of Japanese tourists much of the year. I camp at the Hilton for three nights to wait for Nida to dissipate.

The final leg of the trip is 1,730 nm from Guam to Seoul, South Korea. The route crosses the southern part of Honshu, tracks above the Sea of Japan, and up the Korean Peninsula. I've flown this leg before, and though I've never encountered the spectacular headwinds our bomber crews witnessed during World War II, I'm careful to top every tank, just in case.

Good thing. I climb out of Guam at 8 a.m. with clear skies forecast most of the way to Korea. I'm surprised to find a slight push at 6,000 feet, again nudging the Caravan toward 150 knots. Piece of cake, I think with foolish optimism.

I make landfall at Kushimoto, Japan, just after sunset, cross the island of Honshu and run headlong into exactly the headwinds I was afraid of. As I start out into the Sea of Japan, groundspeed drops to 130, then 120, 110, and finally to 100 knots. I stagger on toward Seoul, concerned but not alarmed about fuel.

The air data computer on the Chelton suggests I'm fighting 60-knot headwinds. My speed finally stabilizes between 90 and 100 knots for the last four hours into Seoul. I'm forced to climb to 8,000 feet across southern South Korea to comply with the MEA, and at that level, I'm reduced to only 90 knots for the final hour of the trip.

What was planned as a 12-hour leg turns into 14 hours for an average speed of 124 knots, the slowest hop of the trip. Thank God for Ziploc bags.

There must be easier ways to make a living, I muse, as I feather the prop and shut down the big PT6A turbine for the last time. The roar out front spools down to a whimper, I pop the door, drop the boarding ladder, and climb down to Korea. Seoul is cold, about minus 10 degrees Celsius compared to Guam at 25 degrees Celsius this morning.

A day later, I ride a Korean Airlines 747 home to Los Angeles in 11 hours even. Somehow, it doesn't seem fair.

17

The Flight(s) of Pink Lady

In Alaska, airplanes truly can take on any mission.

The sound is unmistakable.

Today, I'd recognize that sound in the first two seconds, but 50 years ago, it was totally alien to me. It was high-pitched and guttural at the same time; the smooth, even roar of a gasoline-powered monster, a 1,650-hp supernova on a leash.

The first time I heard it, I was busy finding and putting out root fires far north of the Arctic Circle in Alaska, about 300 miles from any place with a name you might recognize. (You have heard of Anaktuvuk Pass, haven't you?) I was part of a fire crew mopping up after a forest fire in the southern Brooks Range. It was about 9 p.m., but the sun was still up, apparently delighted at shining all day and what would normally be all night.

The fierce sound grew in intensity, mechanical love made audible, even more so when its source became obvious. It was a 12-cylinder Merlin engine, busily converting fuel to noise in a P-51 Mustang, coming straight at me. The pilot was flat-hatting at about 50 feet AGL, probably terrifying the local Grizzlies and Caribou and happily consuming sky at perhaps 350 mph.

"Thank you, God" I thought, as the Mustang sliced past me and pulled up into a glorious chandelle, then dived back down for another pass. It didn't go unnoticed that the entire airplane was painted bright pink, and I caught a flash of the name *Pink Lady* stenciled beneath the barely PG-rated nose art.

For a college kid on summer vacation from the University of Alaska, the *Pink Lady* was a brief but welcome respite from a 12-hour day of hard work. I was looking for wisps of smoke in the above-ground root structure of burned-out trees in the permafrost of the local muskeg. One of four students who'd elected to fight fires May through late September, I was trying to scratch up enough money to pay for the fall semester.

For a college kid on summer vacation from the University of Alaska, the Pink Lady *was a brief but welcome respite from a 12-hour day of hard work.*

I learned later that this particular Mustang had been sold as surplus after World War II, then was somehow reacquired by the government when the Bureau of Land Management needed a recon airplane to help coordinate firefighting. The bureau had about a dozen airplanes at work during the summer fire season, mostly amphibious singles and twins dedicated to positioning fire crews as close as possible to fires.

The Mustang helped coordinate with base on crew and equipment needs, and because it was so fast, it could oversee three or four fires a day to help locate hot spots, relay requests for additional equipment or personnel, and generally position and help manage the needs of fire-fighting crews. If the bureau needed more range, the airplane had hard points beneath the wings to mount aux tanks.

Over the next three months, I hung around the Fairbanks fire base in hopes that I might find an opportunity to snag the rear seat on a flight. I almost made it, too. The guy who was supposed to fly observer in the Mustang's rear pit was sick one day, and the bureau preferred to have someone in the *Pink Lady*'s rear seat who knew a little about aviation. I knew as little as anyone, so I stepped up and volunteered. Sadly, the regular observer showed up a few minutes before launch and refused to accept my offer of $50 to discreetly return home and nurse his cold. Bummer.

Like most civilized Mustangs, *Pink Lady* had the rear 85-gallon fuselage tank removed and a tiny, suitably uncomfortable seat installed in its place, no engine or flight controls in back. Just radios, a shoulder harness and a narrow, tapering, bubble canopy to bump your helmet against during one of the best rides you could ask for.

I saw *Pink Lady* perhaps a dozen times over those three summers, and the pilots always gave us ground-pounders a mini-air show, mostly because we were in the middle of nowhere, and there was no one around to tell them they couldn't. Most of the pilots were also war surplus, and they were overjoyed to be allowed to fly a properly maintained Mustang without being shot at.

With support from the P-51, a few ratty DC-3s, three tired and rusty Grumman Gooses (Geese?), a handful of Cessna 180s on floats, and a few other marginally airworthy machines that were older than their pilots, fire crews could stay on scene for up to 10 days, the bureau's legal limit, and boy, were we ready to come home after 10 days in the boonies.

Airplanes handled practically every mission in the Alaskan bush, sometimes para-dropping supplies or smoke jumpers, often transporting firefighters in to the nearest lake, river, or stream (and occasionally, even getting back out without breaking anything), hauling provisions and beer to a tired team in the truly shaggy tundra, and performing other tasks you might not believe. We were frequently amazed at what the Bureau of Land Management airplanes and pilots could do.

Fighting forest fires in Alaska was a little different than in the lower 48. We had no on-scene air support from tankers of any kind, and the dedicated, Canadair CL-215 water bomber was still 10 years in the future, quietly gestating in some designer's brain. The Navstar satellite system (better known as GPS) was also far in the future, so directions to a "smoke" were usually simple; fly 11 miles west of the village of Chiginook and look for the bend in the east/west creek.

There were probably less than 1,000 miles of paved highways in Alaska at that time, but there were many thousands of miles of dirt. During summer after the seasonal rains had come and gone, dust from those roads covered everything. Conversely, most of the ground was permafrost below about a foot or two, so the thaw of late spring/early summer would leave standing water everywhere.

Add to that the fact that the trees had figured out their roots couldn't grow vertically down through the permafrost, so the

We'd sometimes see from the air that [a fire] burned for what must have been a week or more and finally burned itself out after immolating 100,000 acres. There were no satellites looking down on us in those days, so much of the time, no one even knew it had happened.

aforementioned root structure was above the surface. A burned-out tree might still be barbequing itself under the leaves of tundra with roots that snaked 20 feet or more horizontally in all directions. If you didn't cut out every smoking root, you might have to come back later and fight the fire all over.

Lightning often started fires in remote sections of the 586,000 square mile territory/state, and when we flew out to fight a reported fire, we'd sometimes see from the air that another one nearby had burned for what must have been a week or more and finally burned itself out after immolating 100,000 acres. There were no satellites looking down on us in those days, so much of the time, no one even knew it had happened.

Firefighting was such big business in Alaska that every year we had professional firefighters fly in from Canada, Sweden, Norway, and other points international, work through the Alaska dry season, and fly home. These guys were pros, and they were paid accordingly, but their presence was more appreciated than resented.

Sometimes in early fall, when the temperature began to drop precipitously north of the Arctic Circle, we'd find ourselves incongruously fighting fires in light snow. Put all these conditions together, and it led to a popular expression among firefighters: "Alaska is the only place in the world where you can fight a forest fire while standing knee deep in water, coughing from the dust, while the wind blows snow in your face."

On Dogs, and Airplanes, and Alaska

Every March, these dogs provide a vivid demonstration of the joy of life.

It was 1976 and I was returning from Phoenix, Arizona, to Long Beach, California, in my wood-wing Bellanca Cruisemaster after a photo shoot. My best buddy, a 4-year-old Alaskan malamute named Wolf, was asleep in the back seat, and I was determined to make a smooth landing in Long Beach so he wouldn't howl in disapproval.

As I passed Palm Springs, I called Los Angeles radio, and they reported the weather was going down fast in Long Beach. They felt it should remain VFR for another hour, and I'd be there in about 40 minutes, so I wasn't concerned.

Thirty minutes later, when I was nearing the airport, the weather had outrun me. Visibility was 2 miles beneath a 700-foot overcast. Still not a major problem. I was current for IFR and Long Beach was now slightly below VFR minimums.

Also, just to make things more fun, my artificial horizon, the primary IFR instrument, was becoming erratic. Not good, but no reason to panic.

Just about the time I was considering missing the approach and diverting to a different airport, I felt a big, wet doggy tongue licking my right ear.

I couldn't help but laugh. Things weren't that tough, after all. I relaxed, and a few seconds later, my Bellanca popped out the bottom of the overcast and the landing didn't earn any howls of disapproval.

I'll never know if Wolf somehow sensed that things weren't going well and decided it was time for a dog kiss, but whatever his motivation, he earned the biggest rib-eye steak I could find that evening.

When I was a kid, a few years back, I always considered myself lucky to be growing up a government brat. My father was an inspector with the Department of Justice, and we moved around quite a bit. (Standard joke in the family: "My dad has been in and out of jail for 30 years.")

Our most exciting move was to Anchorage, Alaska, when I was 12, and that's where I discovered both airplanes and Siberian huskies, more or less simultaneously. It seemed huskies, Alaskan malamutes, and variations thereof were practically everywhere in Anchorage, and I'm convinced they're the happiest creatures on the planet.

Arctic dog breeds seem to have smiles on their faces most of the time. That's especially true of huskies. They don't wag their tails so much as they rotate them, creating a vortex of extra thrust on the dog sled trails that were more common than roads in those early days. They wave their broad brushes almost continuously when they're racing in the snow, especially when they're pulling a sled. Huskies love to run and cavort in the white of winter, and most of them look even happier when someone shows up with a harness.

A husky seemed a logical pet in Alaska, and I always wanted a husky or a malamute. (I'm now living with my fifth arctic breed, a solid white husky named Kenai who talks a lot. He edits everything I write with howls of approval or yodels of dissent.)

About the same time, I learned that "little" airplanes were/are profuse in America's then-northern territory. Alaska is well over half a million square miles of tundra, mountains, glaciers, lakes, and rivers, roughly a sixth the size of the other 49 states combined and more than twice the size of Texas.

For better or worse, the topography of the far north is so dynamic that there isn't much of a highway network, about on par with that of Vermont.

Not much has changed if you try to get around by car or truck in what is now the 50th state. Juneau, for example, Alaska's capital city on the far southeast coast, is totally isolated by mountains, glaciers, and the Pacific Ocean. There are no roads in or out of Juneau. You either fly in, float in, hike in, or parachute in.

The population density in the state is so low (barely one inhabitant per square mile) that the Alaska Railroad makes frequent stops in the middle of nowhere along its miniscule 500 miles of track to pick up passengers, often one at a time.

Airplanes are mandatory in such a remote location, and accordingly, Alaska has more general aviation aircraft and pilots per capita than any other state. The world's largest seaplane base is located at Lake Hood,

just south of Anchorage. Collectively, Merrill Field and Anchorage International Airport have nearly 1,000 airplanes based locally.

In other words, Alaska is a great place to fly. Add it to your bucket list.

Each year since 1973, airplanes and dogs come together in the first week of March to celebrate the Fur Rendezvous, Anchorage's answer to New Orleans' Mardi Gras. The premier event is what promoters call the toughest race on Earth — the annual 1,000 nm Iditarod Trail Sled Dog Race from Fourth Avenue in downtown Anchorage to Nome, Alaska.

Airplanes are mandatory in such a remote location, and accordingly, Alaska has more general aviation aircraft and pilots per capita than any other state.

The race commemorates the 1927 delivery of anti-toxin serum to stop an outbreak of diphtheria. The winter of 1927 was especially cold and bitter, leaving Nome isolated and nearly inaccessible, far up on the northwest coast of Alaska. The Bering Sea was frozen solid, so delivering the serum by sea wasn't possible.

The aircraft of the day were all open cockpit, and wind chill would probably have been an incomprehensible minus 73 degrees Celsius (minus 100 degrees Fahrenheit), again, not possible. The only viable option was to race northwest over land by dog team. (Snowmobiles were 40 years in the future.)

It was still deep winter in much of central Alaska, and that was, perhaps counter-intuitively, a good thing. The Yukon River, an unobstructed pathway toward Nome, was under snow and frozen solid. For most of the rest of the year, the Iditarod trail would be a near-impassable quagmire of muskeg (tundra and melt water), unusable by dogsleds.

Twenty mushers and 150 dogs relayed the serum over five days, fighting near white-out blizzard conditions and dangerously cold temperatures. Collectively, the mushers and their dogs saved the town of Nome and its outlying villages from an epidemic. The lead dog on the final leg of the relay into Nome, Balto, is honored with a bronze statue in Central Park, New York City.

Today, of course, getting to Nome isn't the challenge it was 90 years ago. Alaska Airlines operates Boeing 737s on a regular schedule, and bush pilots use Nome as a popular base for traveling around the western portion of the state.

Airplanes are involved in practically every aspect of life in Alaska, and that includes the Iditarod race.

Airplanes are involved in practically every aspect of life in Alaska, and that includes the Iditarod race. A fleet of ski-equipped aircraft are stationed along many of the 39 checkpoints of the Iditarod to provide logistic and veterinary support to the contestants and their dogs, plus keep watch over the race in case of emergencies. Veterinarians are stationed at every checkpoint, and others are on call at vet hospitals near the route. Mushers are required to make a total of three rest stops, two for 8 hours each and one for 24 hours.

Support aircraft range from de Havilland Beavers and Twin Otters to the inevitable workaholic Piper Super Cubs and Aviat Huskies. Perhaps surprisingly, even a 90-pound husky or malamute can be partially anesthetized, loaded aboard a Cub or Beaver, and flown out to a nearby veterinary hospital.

Competitors pay a $4,000 fee to enter the race and must qualify by participating in several of Alaska's other sled dog races before they're cleared to enter the Iditarod. First prize is around $50,000, and the remainder of the field splits another $300,000.

Virtually all mushers now carry satellite phones, and since checkpoints are usually no more than 50 miles apart, ski-equipped rescue aircraft are less than an hour away if a dog tears a cruciate or meniscus and needs transport to a hospital directly from the bush.

Veterinarians also caution mushers not to run the dogs too hard so that they breathe in supercooled air, frozen to minus 34 degrees Celsius (minus 30 degrees Fahrenheit) or less. Frosted lungs can kill a dog or a human.

> *If anyone ever doubts there is*
> *a God, they need to look no*
> *further than a dog.*

Similarly, a typical sled dog can burn as much as 10,000 calories a day, so a musher needs to stay ahead of their energy requirements by feeding them regularly on the trail or at the rest stop.

Back in the '50s, downtown Anchorage was always the starting line of the race. Early every March, we looked forward to the jubilant sound of perhaps 500 huskies, eager to test themselves against the elements. They could be heard everywhere in town, and those of us with a penchant for their canine poetry always characterized their yodeling howls as the voice of Alaska.

I lived on Third Avenue in those early days, and we could hear the howling for their breakfast or dinner in the days leading up to events leading up to the start of the Iditarod.

Sadly, global warming has recently robbed Anchorage of snow in early March, but the city now trucks in snow from the nearby Chugach Mountains for a ceremonial celebration of the Iditarod's start. The real starting line is somewhere to the north, sometimes as far north as Fairbanks, 300 miles north.

I moved south many years ago, but it seems there's always been a husky in my life. Huskies, and dogs in general, have become steadfast friends, and many of them even condescend to fly with me.

My current 90-pound buddy is the most agreeable animal I've ever known. He loves to fly, probably because he's not confined to a canvas bag. He doesn't complain too much if I make mediocre landing, and like all dogs, he's great company, once you learn his differences.

Dogs see with their nose, they say "Thank you" with their tongue, they laugh with their tail, and they love with all their heart.

If anyone ever doubts there is a God, they need to look no further than a dog.

Curiosity Mars Rover exploring the surface of the red planet.

Flying
Above Mars

You think we have it tough flying here on Earth? Consider the problems of aviating above Mars.

Like most pilots, I've been a major fan of the space program since long before there was one. As a kid, I built models of everything from biplanes to jets. My heroes were Yeager, Hoover, and Crossfield, and I was a voracious reader of anything aviation.

I was also a big fan of science fiction, futuristic stories of exploring the universe. I read Ray Bradbury, Robert Heinlein, Isaac Asimov, Arthur C. Clark, and Frederick Pohl, among others, and hoped that I might someday possess the imagination to emulate them.

In my own little nonfiction world, I've written at least a dozen articles about space travel and the benefits of space technology, and I've been one of NASA's strongest boosters. In 2010, I was the last journalist to "fly" the world's only motion-based space shuttle simulator at NASA headquarters in Houston. A few days later, NASA decommissioned the sim and disassembled it for storage.

Back in the early '80s, when the "journalist-in-space program" was announced, I applied enthusiastically, knowing I had little chance against folks such as Walter Cronkite, Peter Jennings, and Hugh Downs. Whatever my chances might have been, they evaporated with the explosion of Challenger in January 1986 and the death of teacher-in-space Christa McAuliffe and six astronauts.

Still, space exploration remained a fascinating preoccupation. Over the years, I've interviewed astronauts such as Buzz Aldrin, Frank Borman, and Robert "Hoot" Gibson. I've also visited the Kennedy Space Center on Cape Canaveral several times and witnessed a half-dozen launches.

I was probably as enthusiastic about 2012's landing of the Mars rover, Curiosity, as the Jet Propulsion Laboratory scientists who built the one-ton, SUV-sized vehicle. It was truly an amazing triumph, especially considering that Mars is, on average, 150 million miles away. Any command from Earth requires nearly 12 minutes to cover such a distance (traveling at the speed of sound — roughly 186,000 miles per second). The descent from orbit to landing required only six minutes, so the computers aboard Curiosity had to be totally autonomous. They needed to make all their own decisions during the descent and actual touchdown.

They did it pretty well. Curiosity blazed through the thin Martian atmosphere at 13,000 mph, then slowed to land at 1.7 mph. (Curiosity landed right on target in Gale Crater at 1:32 a.m. EDT, August 6, 2012, only one minute behind the schedule NASA had laid out months before.)

Curiosity immediately began the tasks for which it was designed — exploring Mars to answer the big question, "Was there once life on the red planet?"

In pursuit of that goal, I couldn't help wondering how difficult it might be to explore Mars by aircraft — perhaps the most efficient method of examining as much of the surface as possible. By coincidence, the total surface area of Mars is almost exactly equal to the land surface of Earth, so exploring Mars could be a major undertaking.

> *I couldn't help wondering how difficult it might be to explore Mars by aircraft, perhaps the most efficient method of examining as much of the surface as possible. Not too surprisingly, NASA was way ahead of me.*

Not too surprisingly, NASA was way ahead of me. The idea is far from new. Nearly a half-century ago, the late Werner Von Braun envisioned landings utilizing hypersonic gliders. NASA's Langley Research Center has been investigating the possibilities for several years, concentrating on a concept called ARES (aerial regional-scale environmental surveyor), a rocket-powered system that would maneuver a mile above the planet at 400 mph until it runs out of fuel.

NASA isn't sure the concept is viable, but it's continuing to investigate the possibilities for a future mission. NASA scientists would love to come up with an aircraft that could explore all the impressive geologic features on the planet, especially Valles Marineris, the 2,500-mile-long, 30,000-foot-deep canyon that makes Earth's Grand Canyon look like a road rut.

Flying on Mars is an intriguing challenge, especially to a pilot who's been operating above Earth for the last 60 years. Mars is a much smaller planet, so gravity is only about 37% of the standard 1g here on Earth. Lifting the weight of a research aircraft would be far less of a problem on Mars than it is here.

Unfortunately, that's about the only benefit of aviating above Mars. The typical Martian atmosphere is extremely thin — about 6 millibars, less than 1% of Earth's protective shield. At a representative ground level (there are no seas on Mars), it's roughly the equivalent density of the Earth's sky 100,000 feet above sea level.

That means any form of aircraft might need very large lifting surfaces, and stall speeds would be extremely high, just to remain aloft. Such realities would demand an imaginative takeoff and launch mechanism, and controlled landings on the surface of Mars would be nearly impossible because of the high stall speed.

Mars is a much smaller planet, so gravity is only about 37 percent of the standard 1g force here on Earth. Lifting the weight of a research aircraft would be far less of a problem on Mars than it is here. Unfortunately, that's about the only benefit of aviating above Mars.

Several concepts have been considered for Mars-capable research aircraft, and they would almost certainly be unmanned drones rather than manned vehicles. One was a series of small, expendable gliders, launched from orbit. These could enter the atmosphere as capsules, descend to a reasonable altitude, leave their cocoons, deploy wings and a tail, reconnoiter, and photograph specific areas of interest. They'd then transmit the information back to an orbiting mother ship before landing and perhaps serving as miniature science platforms after touchdown, assuming they survive the crash.

There's nothing even close to a natural runway on Mars, as the surface is strewn with boulders, craters, and mountains. Considering the cost to send a pound of payload to Mars, deliberately designing expendable aircraft seems like a bad idea.

Accordingly, another option might be entomopters — small, reusable aircraft that would generate lift similar to insects on Earth. Unlike airplanes or birds, insects develop lift by the continuous creation of and shedding of vortices on their wings. Such vortex formation and shedding produces very high lift coefficients, roughly five times more efficient than conventional aircraft airfoils.

This allows insects to take off, maneuver, hover, and land vertically. If such techniques could be applied to a miniature Martian aerial rover, possibly by blowing air out from the trailing edges of the wings (though conventional wings, as we know them, might not be practical in such a thin atmosphere), a much smaller flapping-wing aircraft, perhaps 1 meter in span, could take off, fly a photo reconnaissance mission, and return to the mother ship without concern for air density.

Of course, Mars' atmosphere is almost pure carbon dioxide with no oxygen, so any flying machine would need to bring along its own oxygen supply or use an alternate power source for combustion. The obvious options would be solar or nuclear power. Most previous Mars ground-exploration rovers (especially the two most recent, Spirit and Opportunity) employed solar power but were plagued with dust storms that covered the solar panels with sand and reduced charging capability to near zero.

Additionally, a solar-powered flying machine would require major amounts of power, perhaps incompatible with solar energy sources, especially for a planet so far from the sun.

The Curiosity probe used nuclear power — a radioisotope, thermoelectric, plutonium dioxide that will be unaffected by dust storms and could provide energy for as long as 14 years. A similar system might be utilized by a Martian aircraft.

Another limiting factor on Mars might be the temperature. The fourth planet from the sun is half again as far out in space as Earth, and it's proportionately colder. The average temperature on Mars is about minus 60 degrees Celsius, though it may reach 20 degrees Celsius during the day at the equator. The temperature at the poles may drop to minus 120 degrees Celsius. Such realities would demand very resilient operating systems plus a heater to protect any form of aircraft.

Cosmic radiation would also pose a special problem, even for an unmanned robotic system, carrying nothing more than gas sensors, cameras, and instrumentation. Shielding would be mandatory for any aircraft flying above the surface of the planet. Solar radiation could effectively fry critical systems of an aircraft flying above Mars.

Navigation would be a challenge, too. The planet has no magnetic field, so there'd be no convenient way to determine north or any other direction. Without several satellites overhead, there'd obviously be no GPS guidance, though a form of ADF provided by the mother ship might work over short distances. Other possible methods of navigation might include a modified version of inertial or celestial guidance. Similarly, a downlink might be utilized from satellites orbiting overhead, commanding relative bearings toward a given destination by tracking position with reference to photogrammetric landmarks.

General aviation rarely receives credit for all the missions it performs — cargo, air ambulance, firefighting, aerial survey, law enforcement, pipeline and power line patrol, wildlife management, and about a hundred other jobs. Wouldn't it be interesting if the first Martian aerial rover reconnaissance vehicle turned out to be a descendant of the Skyhawk?

20

Attired in training versions of their shuttle launch and entry suits, STS-133 commander Steve Lindsey, pilot Eric Boe (background), and mission specialists Tim Kopra (right foreground) and Alvin Drew participate in a simulation exercise in the motion-base shuttle mission simulator in the Jake Garn Simulation and Training Facility at NASA's Johnson Space Center. NASA Photo by James Blair.

We Fly the Space Shuttle – Simulator, That Is

I never got into space, but for a while in 1990, I sure didn't know the difference.

I always seem to be in the wrong time warp. I was born too late to fly fighters in World War II and too early for the space program. Like so many other young pilots, I desperately wanted to make it to space, but that was not to be.

Back in the early '80s, I applied for the journalist-in-space program and was advised I'd made the first cut, which narrowed the field from something like 20,000 applicants to about 2,000. Unfortunately, as noted in Chapter 19, when teacher Christa McAuliffe was lost in the explosion of the Challenger in 1986, that was the end of all programs to fly a civilian into space.

Later, I wrote to NASA twice, requesting a chance to fly the space shuttle motion-based simulator, and was turned down both times because of the heavy sim-flight schedule. NASA was busy training pilots for the real thing, and there was little time remaining for journalists.

A few years later, I met retired astronaut Robert "Hoot" Gibson, and mentioned my dream of perhaps someday flying the space shuttle simulator. Gibson is a not-so-old pro in the astronaut business. In addition to making five flights in the shuttle and spending over a month in space, Gibson was chief of the astronaut office in the mid-'90s, and he felt there might be a chance for my flight now that the shuttle program was winding down.

There was only one motion-based shuttle simulator, and it was at NASA's Johnson Space Center in Houston, Texas. Though NASA is no longer training crews since the shuttle program was terminated, the agency kept the sim up and running for recurrent training and emergency-procedure practice.

My opportunity to fly what may be the ultimate simulator came in late June of 1990. I traveled to Houston, and Gibson flew down from his home in Tennessee to oversee my experience and make certain I didn't break anything.

In Houston, Gibson introduced me to Flight Director Paul Dye. Like Gibson, Dye is a confirmed aviation nut. In addition to serving as flight director on 37 shuttle flights, Dye is a member of EAA with a Van's RV-8 and an RV-3. He agreed to monitor my efforts on the shuttle simulator and was the perfect host at NASA. Dye is probably one of the most knowledgeable and proficient sim aviators at NASA, and his advice and counsel were invaluable.

Gibson explained that the sim is very accurate in reproducing the response of the actual space shuttle, and he should know. Like all of the astronauts who train as pilots, Gibson is a former military fighter pilot with thousands of hours in fighters. He's made literally thousands of approaches in the full-motion-based simulator and in NASA's highly modified Gulfstream G-2s, better known as the shuttle training aircraft. NASA operated four of the 1970-era jets, all heavily modified to simulate the shuttle's brick-like glide path during the last 35,000 feet of the approach.

The shuttle is unquestionably the world's least efficient, most expensive, and fastest glider. It's also the most complicated machine ever built: a quarter-million pounds empty with some 2.5 million parts. The simulator doesn't quite match that level of complexity, but it does an excellent job of reproducing real in-flight response in a ground-bound cockpit.

The flight deck is familiar, yet foreign, with eight flat-panel PFD/MFD displays that offer graphical presentations of many standard aviation parameters — airspeed, altitude, attitude, heading, rate of climb — plus a number of other instruments you probably wouldn't recognize. Still, there's enough that's friendly so that those of us confined to the bottom 10 miles of sky don't feel lost.

Climbing into either of the pilot seats is exactly that — a climb, and I was doing it in comfortable street clothes with the cockpit conveniently straight and level as opposed to lying on its back. It's hard to imagine how difficult the task would be wearing a full David Clark pressure suit with the aircraft pointed vertically up.

The pilot flies the shuttle with a short-throw, fly-by-wire hand controller mounted on a pedestal. It looks fairly conventional, but it has at least one function you may not recognize. It incorporates a third direction of travel in addition to pitch and roll.

In space, without the benefit of an atmosphere, the shuttle can be maneuvered through its yaw axis, and the pilot commands thrusters to accomplish a lateral yaw roll by simply twisting the stick. This fires thrusters that rotate the spacecraft as if it were balanced on the head of a pin. Pretty obviously, that function isn't operative during an approach to landing.

Launch from Cape Canaveral

Everyone aboard the shuttle is a passenger during launch, as the entire process — liftoff to orbit — is computer-controlled. Dye nevertheless gave us a taste of the launch. The first step in a simulated launch is to rotate the sim to the aforementioned vertical position. This is, after all, a motion-based simulator, so we were given an idea of the real starting position, lying on our backs.

The simulator re-creates the experience of launch fairly accurately, though Gibson comments that the vibration of an actual launch is exponentially more violent than the sim experience. Considering that the sim is primarily an electric device with hydraulic assist, repeated shaking wouldn't be conducive to long life.

You feel the rumble of the engines seven seconds before launch, and when the countdown reaches zero and the explosive bolts release the shuttle, the launch becomes a numbers game, and all the numbers are *big*.

You can watch the tower begin to flash by as the 4.4 million-pound "stack" starts its climb with the assistance of about 7.5 million pounds of thrust. The stack consists of the orbiter itself, two solid rocket boosters (SRBs), and the huge external tank.

Gibson commented that the real shuttle comes off the ground with what seems like a tidal wave of power. Acceleration is analogous to the thrust of a giant rubber band, subjecting the crew to an eventual $3g$ of vertical acceleration. Meanwhile, the massive thrust of five rocket engines creates a level of vibration reminiscent of a huge, berserk, paint-shaking machine.

Eight seconds into the flight, the shuttle bites back. It begins a roll program, rotating onto its back and climbing away from Florida as if its tail is on fire, which, by the way, it is. The shuttle's flight path becomes as much horizontal as vertical as it climbs higher, accelerating and gaining altitude almost exponentially. Zero airspeed to Mach 1 takes less than 60 seconds, and you can watch as the speed and altitude climb at an increasing rate. As you monitor the digital readout, you'll see numbers you've never seen before.

At two minutes, the shuttle is passing through Mach 4 (about 2,800 mph) and is already climbing through 150,000 feet. At this point, the spacecraft is burning about 60,000 gallons of fuel a minute. Looking out the side windows, you'll see the flash of the SRBs shutting down and separating from the stack. The SRBs parachute down and land in the Atlantic, where they're retrieved for use on a future launch. Now, the shuttle is flying on its three main engines, still burning fuel from the giant external tank.

At five minutes, I glance out the small, left window to see what I'm told is the outline of the Chesapeake Bay drifting by below. The simulator's depictions of Earth aren't very realistic, but they don't need to be, as astronaut trainees have little use for the outside display. Considerations of IFR and VFR become irrelevant in an aircraft designed to operate outside the Earth's atmosphere.

At just under 9 minutes after launch and 75 miles above the Earth (roughly 400,000 feet), the main engines shut down and the orange tank is ejected at the equivalent of Mach 25. The shuttle continues to coast uphill at 500 feet per second to orbit. In total, the shuttle's climb to altitude requires 45 minutes, and all but the first 9 minutes are without power — basically coasting uphill. Once established in orbit, the shuttle circles the Earth every hour and a half in a typical orbit at 180 miles above the planet.

Return to Earth

At the conclusion of the orbital flight, the shuttle begins the reentry process in what most pilots would consider an unusual manner. For several good reasons, the spacecraft typically flies in space upside down and backward with reference to the Earth.

The most important reason is that flying backward with the engines in the rear provides the crew with maximum protection from micrometeorites and space debris. Second, all the windows on the shuttle are on the top of the fuselage, and since there's no up or down in space, it's logical to fly inverted to orient the windows toward Earth. Third, those 34,000 heat-shielding silica tiles on the belly of the aircraft help protect the crew from the heat of the sun, no longer filtered through the atmosphere. In the direct light of the sun in orbit OAT in space can rise to 121 degrees Celsius (250 degrees Fahrenheit).

The deorbit process begins with a 3-minute burn of the orbital maneuvering system (OMS) engines, slowing orbital velocity by about 200 mph. This slows orbital speed to a mere 17,000 mph, not enough to keep the spacecraft in orbit, and the shuttle slowly begins to descend. To manage the reentry, the computer maneuvers the spacecraft through a half

Astronauts Frederick H. (Rick) Hauck, left, STS-26 commander, and Richard O. Covey, pilot, man their respective stations in the shuttle mission simulator (fixed base) at the Johnson Space Center. A simulation for their anticipated June 1988 flight aboard the space shuttle Discovery began October 20, 1987. Astronaut David C. Hilmers, one of three mission specialists for the flight, is partially visible in the foreground. NASA photo

somersault to fly belly down, nose forward — the equivalent of straight and level. (The commander or pilot can fly the full reentry if necessary, but most of the time, the computer will do a more accurate job.)

As the spacecraft begins to fall back into the atmosphere, the computer gradually brings the nose up to a 40-degree angle of attack to let the ceramic tiles on the belly absorb the heat of reentry. The speed slowly bleeds off as the aircraft begins to encounter thicker air. The wings gradually assume more lift, and the computer commands a series of four aero-braking turns at up to 70 degrees of bank to slow the spacecraft and continue the descent, meanwhile maintaining the 40-degree pitch attitude. These turns are intended to help dissipate speed without overheating the tiles, subjected to temperatures of 1,500 degrees Celsius during reentry. After the final aero-braking turn, the computer levels the wings and lowers the nose, and what was once a spacecraft becomes an aircraft once again.

If you guessed the shuttle makes a terrible glider, you guessed right. Most pilots had better hope they never come close to experiencing the glide characteristics of a space shuttle. My Mooney and most other general aviation aircraft come downhill power-off at about 10-to-1 lift-to-drag: 10 feet forward for every foot of descent. When I earned my glider rating 40 years ago, I flew a Czechoslovakian LET L-13 Blaník trainer that offered a glide ratio of roughly 28-to-1. The most efficient high-performance sailplanes record ratios as high as 70-to-1.

In contrast, the shuttle's glide at high altitude is barely distinguishable from that of a grand piano. The spacecraft experiences a variable glide ratio because it operates in variable levels of air density. It's a spacecraft in space and a conventional aircraft in air (duh!) so its glide characteristics change as the air becomes thicker. At hypersonic velocities in the upper atmosphere, above about Mach 5 and 200,000 feet, the shuttle glides at a 1-to-1 ratio, 1 foot forward travel for each foot of descent, about the same as the aforementioned Steinway. That increased to 2-to-1 at supersonic velocities and improves to about 4.5-to-1 when you're on final approach.

In contrast to the extreme nose-up-attitude of reentry, the world's largest glider must assume a nose-down pitch for the last 50,000 feet of descent. During this phase of the shuttle's approach, it's dropping out of the sky at 10,000 fpm. Pilot error makes an undershoot possible, but the computer flies the airplane down to about 50,000 feet before the commander or pilot assumes control. In theory, the pilot takes over just before the shuttle reaches the HAC (heading alignment cone) that's located about 50,000 feet above the Kennedy Space Center.

From there, the shuttle flies directly to a cone of airspace above the threshold of Kennedy's 3-mile-long runway high above the Cape. The approach is similar to a circular pattern. From there, the pilot flies the aircraft around an arcing turn to final approach.

Flying the approach is simplified somewhat by the HUD (head-up display) that overlays the windshield. The HUD allows you to look through the display at the runway and still receive visual cues of the approach. The HUD presents the pilot with a round, green flightpath marker representing the shuttle, and a guidance diamond. Theoretically, if you fly the flightpath marker on top of the guidance diamond at all times, the STS will slide right down final to a squeaker landing — it says here.

Follow the HUD precisely and it will arc you around to final approach at 12,000 feet, 6 miles out, about a minute from touchdown. A 20-degree glideslope can be as steep as a normal ILS, so if you try to fly the approach visually without the help of the HUD, you'll be challenged, to say the least. In the shuttle, you'll be dropping out of the sky at 1,000 feet every six seconds, a pretty ferocious descent rate. In his capacity as unofficial shuttle sim test pilot, Dye has flown many pure VFR approaches to Edwards AFB where the dry lake precedes the actual runway, and Dye has learned to do it reasonably well. For the rest of us, don't try this at home.

As you descend through 2,000 feet at roughly 300 knots glide speed, a pair of triangles begins to rise from the bottom, one on each side of the H, and Gibson suggested I'd better not let them get ahead of me. "That's your flare indicator," he explained. "If you don't catch the rising triangles and begin your flare before they reach the middle of the HUD, you're going to be low, and, of course, you don't have any power to recover."

I learned that lesson on my fifth approach. I flew my first three approaches to the Kennedy Space Center and managed to plant the airplane on the runway all three times, though not necessarily with style or grace.

One of the parameters NASA uses to evaluate a pilot's ability to land the shuttle is gear g-load at touchdown. I received a printout of my landing results at the conclusion of two hours in the sim and noted that the max allowable sink rate was 9 fps, or 540 fpm. My worst effort was about 8.1 fps, barely within tolerance. My best effort of the five successful touchdowns was 3.5 fps — not bad but not exactly graceful.

On my second approach to Edwards AFB, however, I blew it completely. I missed the rise of the flare indicators and wound up too low with no way to recover. (Remember, there's no power for recovery.) I landed short, and the simulator simply locked up. Gibson, always the ultimate diplomat, laughed and reminded me that landing short at Edwards is no major sin as the runway is fronted by several miles of flat lakebed.

You typically come across the fence at 220-230 knots, but again, the speed is masked slightly if you're flying the HUD. Just as with an airliner, the nonflying pilot calls out radar altitude as the commander eases the shuttle down to the runway. His goal is to touch down 2,500 feet past the threshold.

At touchdown, the nose is still high above the runway. During initial flight tests in the late '70s, pilot John Young experimented with holding the nose off as long as possible to maximize aerodynamic braking. Eventually, it was decided to lower the nose earlier to minimize the load on the nose gear. The runway at Kennedy is 3 miles long and the one at Edwards is 5 miles in length, not counting the lakebed, so there's a little fudge factor if you're long. Just don't be short.

After all three wheels are on the asphalt, the pilot deploys the drag chute and applies the brakes to "maintain the center line, so the media will have a photogenic subject," said Gibson. Just as with the real aircraft, there's a certain letdown when you're stopped on the runway at Kennedy or Edwards. But at least in the sim you have the satisfaction of knowing you just landed a near-exact replica of the world's fastest and highest-flying spacecraft.

21

The Joy of Night

It's a slightly esoteric joy but flying at night can be strangely satisfying.

Tonight I fly in my own sensory deprivation chamber, a semi-anechoic capsule seemingly isolated from reality. The sun rolled down beneath the Earth hours ago, leaving me in a blackness well beyond merely dark. It seems there is no outside light above or below, forward or aft, left or right.

I am suspended in an obsidian void of nothing. My little cocoon of darkness flies into the wind at 170 knots, an overcast blocks out stars, and the mostly uninhabited northwest Texas swallows what little illumination might otherwise join together to suggest there is an Earth below. The regular subdued flicker of my strobes startles the night as if to confirm that I am truly alone.

My tiny universe seems to end at my airplane's spinner and wingtips. Like the enigma of a tree falling in the forest without sound, if you fly through a pitch-black sky and there seems to be no Earth below, is it really still there?

> *My tiny universe seems to end at my airplane's spinner and wingtips. Like the enigma of a tree falling in the forest without sound, if you fly through a pitch-black sky and there seems to be no Earth below, is it really still there?*

On the panel in front of me, my artificial world consists of 22 instruments and six radios backlit in pale red, reassuring me that I'm not really alone. They allege I'm somewhere near Wichita Falls and Amarillo, friends from long ago, wisely sleeping in the cold night of late autumn.

The altimeter suggests I'm 12,500 feet above sea level, a meaningless number since the nearest sea is 600 nm away in Baja, California. More relevant, the chart indicates I'm 8,500 feet above this section of West Texas.

131

Outside my insignificant airplane, the sky acknowledges the coming of winter, minus 21 degrees Celsius, but with the cold overcast comes a velveteen smooth passage that's long forgotten summer's uncomfortable turbulence. My headset further isolates me from reality, allowing only a distant background hum to invade my senses.

The heading bug covers 286 degrees on the HSI, and the GPS falls back on those famous explorers, latitude and longitude, to advise that I'm only 286 nm from tonight's destination of Santa Fe, New Mexico.

Other instruments collectively counsel me not to make any mistakes in the dark. My airplane's totalizer (which always sounded like some kind of Star Wars laser weapon or something from one of those movies by Schwarzenegger) warns that I have only 38 gallons remaining before I'll need to return to Earth — black or not, seen or unseen. Fortunately, even flying into a characteristic head wind — assuming I'm actually moving — I will need only two hours' fuel at 11 gph.

How much darker if I just kill the master electrical power switch? I do, inconveniently forgetting that the autopilot will quit without power. Of course, it does, and I quickly apologize to God and flip the master back on.

Looking out at the West Texas plains, or at least, where they should be, I wonder if I'm anywhere near absolute dark. Just for fun, I turn the panel light rheostat all the way to the left, right next to "off." Not dark enough. I turn the instrument lights completely off. Still too much residual light. Not absolute darkness. Not the bottom of Carlsbad Caverns during a power failure. How much darker if I just kill the master electrical power switch?

I do, inconveniently forgetting that the autopilot will quit without power. Of course, it does, and I quickly apologize to God and flip the master back on. At the same time, as if determined to frustrate my search for full opaque, I suddenly fly out from beneath the overcast to a recognizable world resplendent with stars. No moon tonight to ruin the mood.

Almost simultaneously, lights begin to appear below, eager to compete. The terrain also rises, spoiling my search for visual absolute zero. The sky is polished smooth by the wind, and I drift along as if on rails. Somewhere down below, in fact pretty much everywhere down below, the plains of Texas give way to the hard hills and mountains of eastern New Mexico.

Off to the south, I see the gentle glow of Albuquerque highlighting the Sandia and Manzano mountains. To the north, the Sangre de Cristo

Piper Aerostar owned by Gary Evans (*www.texasaviationlaw.com*). Photo by Andrew Broadfoot (*www.andrewbroadfootphotography.com*).

Mountains, the southern terminus of the Rockies, angle down out of high Colorado with snow-capped peaks pointing the way to Aspen, Leadville, and Telluride.

At 60 miles, Santa Fe announces itself as a half-halo of dim light behind higher terrain. In apparent protest of my search for ultimate dark, lights begin to appear everywhere as I approach the city.

Straight ahead, far in the distance, I see a cluster of disembodied lights that seem to float above me. Perhaps a flight of aliens escaped from Roswell? No, it's just the suspended illumination of Los Alamos, where the first nuclear weapon was developed in the 1940s. Perhaps enigmatically, the city looks down on high New Mexico from its station 8,500 feet up. The lack of light between Santa Fe and Los Alamos gives the Atomic City the illusion of being suspended in space.

At 40 miles, I see the lights of Santa Fe itself, hunkered against the side of a mountain, shivering from the cold wind of a late November storm now past, but not before coating the high plains with the first snow of the season.

Santa Fe, for me a town of things remembered, is the quintessential "Olde West," home of the Santa Fe trail of gold rush days. Santa Fe is steeped in 19th century tradition. The city embraces its heritage, a cross between American and Mexican folklore. Silver-mounted turquois is the jewelry of choice, the Santa Fe Plaza is home to numerous Southwest festivals, and huge sombreros are the favored hats. Until a few years ago, Santa Fe had an ordinance that clung to tradition by insisting that all new buildings had to be of adobe construction to maintain the city's image as the "real" Southwest. Even in November, it is a world of tourists below.

The star-shaped airport for the capital city perches on a mesa south of town, 6,300 feet above sea level. In summer, it can be a fierce opponent for those uninitiated in the hazards of high density altitude. Santa Fe can be especially hazardous because terrain climbs higher in three of four directions.

Too many years ago for most pilots my age to remember, I was No. two for takeoff behind a tired-looking, tuna-tanked, Air National Guard Cessna 310 on Santa Fe's Runway 02. My wife and I were on our way home to California after a visit with her parents. It was July hot, and the 310 ahead of us departed, climbed several hundred feet, then apparently lost all power on his right engine, and began to sink back toward the horizon. I watched it slowly descend, then, gradually drop below the opposite end of the runway as the pilot fought a losing battle to keep it in the air. It finally disappeared into a cloud of dust off the end of 02.

I learned later the pilot had flown the airplane into a sand berm off the end of the runway, but the impact was gentle, there was no fire, and all three occupants walked away, though the airplane was totaled. I was next in line for takeoff on an adjacent runway, and I hurried the controller to release me. I was afraid my nervous in-laws might call the tower and tell the controller to have their idiot son-in-law in the Bellanca bring their daughter back to the ramp, so they could send her home to Los Angeles in a sensible Greyhound rather than have her fly home in one of those "little" airplanes. Fortunately, I got away clean.

I touch down with a reassuring squeak, taxi to the ramp, check for angry in-laws, and rejoice in the fact that once again, science and technology have triumphed over fear and superstition.

Tonight, density altitude is well below field elevation as I flip on the landing lights at 10 miles, call the tower, and set up for a wide right base to Runway 33. I touch down with a reassuring squeak, taxi to the ramp, check for angry in-laws, and rejoice in the fact that once again, science and technology have triumphed over fear and superstition.

Three Mistakes I Lived to Write About

If you fly long enough, you'll inevitably make some errors. Here are three I was fortunate to survive.

The Time I Failed Altimeter Class

I'd just dropped the keys and logbooks for the new Caravan on the South African Cessna dealer's desk when his phone rang. He answered it and motioned me to sit. He spoke for a few seconds, then said, "Well, he just walked into my office," and commented, "It's for you."

"Bill, this is Wilfred Otto at Henschel Flugzeug Piper in Kassel, Germany."

I answered and Wilfred said, "Hope you had a good trip in from Florida. What are your plans now?"

I told him I'd be catching the first flight I could find headed back to California.

"How'd you like to fly back to Florida, pick up the very first production Piper Mirage in Vero Beach instead, and ferry it to me in Kassel?"

Silly question. Four hours later, I was sitting in a British Airways 747, lifting off from Johannesburg for London with connections to Orlando. Two days after that, I fired up the first customer's Mirage in Lakeland and launched for Bangor, Maine. It was mid-January and, just as on the Caravan trip a week earlier, Maine was in the grip of a minus 34-degree Celsius cold snap. Of course, Bangor was totally dark when I arrived. At least the weather was decent, though it was bitterly cold.

When I turned onto the 45 inbound to the Bangor Airport and selected gear down, the left main and nose wheel extended normally, but the right main refused to lock green/down. Probably just a little stiff in the frigid, winter sky of northern Maine, I reasoned. I tried cycling the wheels several times, but the right main gear stubbornly refused to lock down. I advised the tower of my problem and asked for a low altitude flyby to verify where the right gear was in its cycle.

The tower reported that the right gear looked to be about three-quarters down but definitely was not locked.

Hmmm. I wasn't about to put Mr. Otto's premier Mirage on its belly, or worse, try to bounce it on the left main gear and hope the right would obligingly swing out and lock down of its own accord.

As I droned around a few miles from the airport, trying to think of something clever, I remembered a story I'd heard at Oshkosh a few years before about a pilot in a warbird who'd had a similar problem and had reasoned his way out of the situation. In that case, it was the left gear that refused to lock into position. The pilot had tried the emergency procedure without success and was faced with a similar situation to mine.

Since the wheels extended outboard, he theorized that he needed to find a way to "g" the airplane in a manner that would exert a down load to push the left main gear toward the wingtip. The only way he could do that was to put the airplane into a left, semi-knife-edge attitude, then slam the top (right) rudder to the floor. That would cause the airplane to yaw hard right, but since attitude was already in a vertical left knife-edge, the result would be a down load on the left main gear that might help push the left wheel outboard toward the low wingtip.

He tried this trick several times, and to his utter amazement, it worked. The left gear light finally blinked on, and the pilot saved the situation by landing the warbird safely. Accordingly, I decided to try the same technique on the new Mirage. I banked hard right, established a near-90-degree bank and slammed the top (left) rudder to the floor. The nose arced hard up, but still no right gear light. I tried it six times, punching the top rudder as hard as I could, and the right, green, gear light finally flicked on.

Convinced that I was now a full-fledged superhero, I called the tower, returned to Bangor airport, and landed normally. Once on the ground, I taxied to the FBO, ordered fuel, and advised the desk manager that I'd be back in the morning for some maintenance.

Next day, the service manager's first question was, "Did you come in nonstop from Florida?" When I answered "Yes," he smiled and said he'd seen the problem before.

"We use a different kind of gear lubricant for the extreme cold temperatures we encounter in Maine, and that usually solves the problem," he told me.

They'd towed "my" Mirage into the shop two hours before I'd arrived, so the airplane was up to room temperature. Next, they put it on jacks, lifted it off the floor, lubed the gear, and cycled it several times.

Everything worked perfectly, of course. The crucial test would come at my next stop, Goose Bay, Labrador, Canada, where I knew it would be even colder than at Bangor.

Sure enough, when I arrived at Goose Bay that afternoon, the temp was closer to minus 40 degrees Celsius, not an uncommon occurrence in deep winter at 61 degrees north. I held my breath and flipped the gear switch to the down position, praying for three green lights.

Again, no right green. OK, at least this time, I had a rough idea of a trick that might work as it had in Bangor. I advised the tower and turned back out of the pattern away from the lights of Goose Bay Airport to see if I could get some assistance from gravity.

If the folks in Bangor had been right about the nature of the problem, i.e. extreme cold temperatures, the same technique should work a second time.

Roll hard right, push hard top rudder. Nothing. Try again, still nothing. Again, no reaction. Again and again. Finally, after 10 progressively more violent and frustrated stabs at the top rudder, the right gear light finally illuminated. I advised the tower that the problem was solved, and the controller immediately cleared me to land.

Nature wasn't quite finished with me, however. The runway had recently been plowed clear of snow, but there was a sheet of ice complicating matters. Just when I thought I was back to normal operation, both main gear brakes turned out to be frozen solid. The airplane touched down normally and immediately began sliding on the ice. Fortunately, I was somewhere near the centerline, so I managed to get it stopped without losing directional control.

Again, I advised the tower of the problem and they notified Woodward Aviation to send out a goat to tow me clear of the runway.

In the shop again the next morning, it was the same diagnosis, extreme cold weather. Woodward, too, lubed the gear, cycled it up and down several times, and pronounced the airplane good to go.

After another day of delay, I finally hit upon a plan that might solve the problem. I filled the 50-gallon ferry tank in the back of the Mirage and filed for FL210 direct Prins Christians Sund (Prince Christian Sound, an NDB on the southernmost tip of the Greenland Icecap), direct Reykjavik Airport (BIRK).

That's just under 1,400 nm, but as usual in winter, the winds at 60 degrees north were wailing at 40-50 knots out of the west up high. With 170 gallons on board, I'd have an easy seven hours' endurance at probably 250 knots groundspeed and a range of 1,750 nm.

I'd been through Iceland several dozen times, often in winter, and I knew the influence of the relatively warm Gulf Stream off the island's west coast kept Iceland unusually warm for a country near the Arctic Circle. Reykjavik rarely saw temperatures colder than minus 18 degrees Celsius (zero degrees Fahrenheit). I decided to fly at normal altitude for most of the trip, then ask ATC for an early descent to warmer air an hour out of Reykjavik to let the gear warm up and preclude any extension problems.

Predictably, the flight went well for the first four hours at 21,000 feet. I called the controller and asked for the lowest altitude he could approve. He dropped me down to 7,000 feet, which put me right in the middle of clouds in the inevitable icing conditions.

The temperature aloft was still very cold, but he advised that the floor of IFR airspace over the ocean was 5,500 feet. I agreed to cancel IFR and report position as I neared the joint U.S./Icelandic air base at Keflavik.

I descended in solid darkness out of the clouds, but there was nothing to see. It was black on black at this time of year as there's hardly any sun to warm things, even at low altitude.

I finally leveled at 1,000 feet and advised the controller that I'd pull back to 2,000 to cross Keflavik and continue to Reykjavik 30 miles further inland along the coast. The temperature was warming nicely 100 miles out of Keflavik. I did notice a slight blue/green tinge to the airspace below. That seemed a little unusual.

Suddenly, it dawned on me what the slight color was. I punched off the autopilot and pulled back hard on the yoke. The Mirage climbed to 2,000 feet in about 30 seconds.

Once my heartbeat dropped back to normal levels, and I fully realized what had almost happened, I called up Iceland Control and asked them for their current altimeter setting.

"November flight, Keflavik altimeter is 28.96."

I'd been flying a few feet above the ocean without knowing it.

When I descended out of FL210 and dropped below 18,000 feet, I'd either forgotten to reset the altimeter from standard to local, or the controller had forgotten to remind me. Either way, it was my error. An altimeter set a full inch too high would translate to a 1,000-foot altitude error. I'd heard about the bioluminescence in ocean waves at night, but I'd never seen it before. Thank God I recognized it this time.

I'll never know how low I was or how close I came to dumping the new Mirage into the ocean, and that's probably just as well. Of course, the gear swung down normally in Reykjavik, and on the following day's flight into Kassel, Germany.

*I'll never know how low I was or
how close I came to dumping the
new Mirage into the ocean, and
that's probably just as well.*

I survived a very stupid and very basic mistake, and you can bet I'll never make that transgression again.

[Editor's Note: In case some readers are confused about altimeter settings — all aircraft operating in positive control airspace (anything above 18,000 feet) must use a standard altimeter setting of 29.92 inches. When an aircraft descends out of 18,000 feet, the pilot switches to the local altimeter setting for the local area. If they fail to do that (as Bill did in this case) and the local altimeter is lower than the high-altitude setting, the airplane may be flying closer to the ground/water than the pilot realizes. The proper altimeter setting is extremely critical for safety in flight.]

The Time I Thought I Was Smarter Than Black Ice

Back in the early '70s, I was in the habit of taking two weeks off at Christmas and flying from California to Venice, Florida, to visit my mom. My wife worked for Douglas Aircraft at the time, and she'd usually file for whatever vacation time she needed to turn what was a 9- to 10-day holiday into 16 days. I was a freelance journalist, so I worked pretty much 24/7, or, as some people believed, I didn't work at all.

In about '73, we loaded up our Bellanca Cruisemaster — a wonderful-handling, wood-and-fabric, four-seat taildragger — and pointed the nose east. As usual, we got off late, stopped in Albuquerque for fuel, and decided to make a short second leg over to Amarillo for the night.

West Texas was living up to its reputation as one of the windiest places on the trip, with frigid winds gusting to 25 from whatever direction was least convenient. I had about 1,000 hours in the Bellanca, and I was unjustifiably confident I could handle whatever was happening ahead.

We arrived over Amarillo just at sunset with the wind blowing a strong left crosswind. Shouldn't be a problem, I reasoned with more bravado than brains as I set up for the landing. Amarillo has wide, comfortable runways, and I was confident I could handle the wind.

About a quarter-mile out on final with the light failing fast, the tower cleared me to land and commented, "We've had reports of black ice on the runway."

I should have been forewarned, but while heard, the message didn't get through. Doesn't sound too tough, I reasoned, as I cross-controlled to maintain the centerline. I touched down 700 feet past the threshold, and in a matter of a second or two, the Bellanca began to weathercock to the left. I tried to correct with full opposite rudder, and eventually hard right brake, but my efforts at directional control seemed to have no effect. Nothing seemed to be working, as the airplane gradually turned a full 180 degrees to the left, seemingly of its own accord, and I basically just hung on. My wife and I were mere passengers in the West Texas wind.

When we finally came to a stop, we were still on the centerline, but facing the opposite direction, with nothing damaged except my pride. The runway was so slick that there had been no side stresses on the airplane. The controller had watched my performance, and commented sarcastically, with a typical Texas drawl, "Bellanca 85N, are you in need of assistance?"

The lesson: "Don't mess with black ice unless you really know what you're doing." Obviously, I didn't.

I'd landed on an asphalt runway covered with black ice. Nothing was broken or even bent, but it required three airport workers, and me manipulating brakes and throttle, to steer a broken path, move the airplane to the ramp, and finally tuck it into a hangar. The lesson: "Don't mess with black ice unless you really know what you're doing." Obviously, I didn't.

The Time I Flew in Like I Was Alone in the World

Perhaps ironically, the next example of dumb behavior occurred the following year on the same 2,000-nm trip to Florida. I'd just had the airplane painted and decided I needed to show it off with a low pass on arrival at Venice.

This time, we got past Lubbock without incident on the first day and stopped at Austin for the night. The following day, I skirted the Gulf Coast to Cross City, Florida, turned south along the coast on one of those Chamber of Commerce days and rode happy tailwinds down to Sarasota. Hoping not to do something dumb in front of Mom, I called Venice Unicom 8 miles out to determine the active runway and check for traffic. I turned west out over the Gulf, then arced back east and lined up for the low pass.

I leveled at 100 feet as I approached the threshold near the beach. There was no one on the radio, and there appeared to be no one in the pattern as I flashed across the numbers — except for a red and white Cherokee departing in the opposite direction. He was just lifting off when I saw him. I pulled up hard and broke right. I had a fleeting glimpse of two very surprised Cherokee drivers as I flew by above them.

My immediate reaction was that the Cherokee pilot was an idiot. Then, I realized there were at least two idiots flying at Venice that after-

My immediate reaction was that the Cherokee pilot was an idiot. Then, I realized there were at least two idiots flying at Venice that afternoon.

noon. Yes, he had departed on the wrong runway without a radio call, but I'd lived in Venice briefly back in the '60s, flown in and out of the airport many times, and I should have remembered there were many NORDO airplanes on the field. Even granted that, I didn't overfly the airport at altitude and make a visual check for traffic before entering the pattern. Not smart.

Fortunately, Mom was late and missed my bird-brain buzz job, so my wife was the only witness to my stupid pilot trick.

I'd like to hope I learned something from these experiences. In the first instance, I was simply too arrogant to admit crosswinds, failing light, and black ice might be too much for me to handle. In the second, the whole idea was ill-advised from start to finish.

I promised never to make those same mistakes twice. I'll just have to find some new ones.

Perspectives From Telluride

Flying never gets old, whether you're a 100-hour baby bird or a 10,000-hour airline eagle. Here's one good reason.

Telluride nestles in a pristine mountain valley elevated nearly 2 miles closer to the sky in southwest Colorado. The surrounding peaks rear up another 3,500 feet above the valley floor on three sides — steep, forested inclines, challenging, and unforgiving to the unknowing.

It is one of the most spectacular alpine venues in the Rockies, ideal for skiing (experts only), breathing, shooting commercials, TV and motion pictures, mountain photography, counting elk, and just plain, uncomplicated living. At 9,000 feet up, only the athletic need apply.

My first visit to this tall paradise was over Christmas break in the mid '60s when I was 50 years more athletic. That trip was in a '63 Austin-Healey 3000, not a bad ride but temporarily attached to Highway 145. At the time, I barely noticed the difference, as the University of New Mexico coeds back in Albuquerque loved that little sports car, and accordingly, so did I.

The city of Telluride lies in a box canyon, and once you travel through the entrance, you find yourself staring up at the marbled peaks high above the valley. Snow had been sparse that winter, and the contrast between seasonal white and solid granite slate only served to emphasize the beauty of the place.

Except there was something missing. Gazing in wonder at the high mountains, I couldn't help speculating about what cinematographers call "the reverse," in this case, looking down rather than up.

Fast forward roughly 50 years and two seasons. I'm looking down on Telluride from 12,500 feet in a new Mooney, the town now rediscovered almost accidently by my Garmin GPS on a homebound flight from Florida. As I make a giant circle around the geographical box, I'm amazed at the change in perspective.

No one has moved the mountains, though most of the snow has retreated to the high peaks, and the town looks pretty much the same as it did back in 1966 — a small, semi-remote hideaway that doubles or triples its population during tourist season. Telluride becomes more laid back in the summer "heat," sometimes as "torrid" as 60 degrees Fahrenheit.

Today, I have the advantage of the real third dimension, not interpreting synthetic vision on a square screen, not translating elevation lines on a chart, but actually witnessing the thrust of the summits at their own level.

Today, I have the advantage of the real third dimension, not interpreting synthetic vision on a square screen, not translating elevation lines on a chart, but actually witnessing the thrust of the summits at their own level. It's late afternoon in Colorado, and this is the true configuration of a Rocky Mountain High (thank you, John Denver). I watch the shadows begin to slant across the valley, and the big pines reaching up for me but falling far short.

This is flying as it should be, unconstrained by the limitations of artificial altitude. Doesn't matter how high you fly. The mere fact of traveling *above* rather than *on* the Earth below is an end in itself.

I rarely travel in non-pilot circles, but when I do, I'm most often asked questions about the difference between airline and general aviation transport. After a half-century of flying in one or another of "those little airplanes," my answer has finally crystalized around the joy of do-it-yourself aviation and the remarkable difference in what you can see from medium-low altitude.

No matter how much faster airline travel may be, typically 200-300 knots quicker than most private aircraft, airlines can never reproduce the same satisfaction considered normal in a Cub, Bonanza, Skyhawk, or Aerostar.

Many have had the passive thrill of walking down a narrow hallway, entering a large, rumbling room, taking a nap, and waking up on the opposite coast or in another country. For those whose flight time has been confined to the often crazed, warped, and dirty window of an airliner, forgive me, but airlines do everything possible to make flying semi-comfortable but unexciting; sometimes convenient, but relatively boring; a group experience rather than an individual experience.

In fact, the major carriers spend millions to provide passengers with entertainment, specifically because there's often not much to see out the window other than slats, flaps, ailerons, and spoilers.

In contrast, a general aviation airplane is more like a flying version of my old Austin-Healey; good visibility straight ahead and behind, to both sides, nearly straight down, and even straight up if you leave the top down, something you can never do in an Airbus or Boeing.

Airline passengers are at a distinct disadvantage of enjoying the view for two major reasons. First, half the Earth's atmosphere resides below 18,000 feet, and that bottom segment contains about 90% of the weather. That means airlines travel above the clouds most of the time. Second, the haze level has gradually risen so high over most of the inhabited world in the last 40 years that, even on a "clear" day, passengers can't see much ground detail from FL300 and up.

Following my first ferry trip in a new Piper Seneca II to the Paris Air Show in 1977, the return flight was an easy one-stop back to Los Angeles. About four hours out, the captain announced over the intercom that we were just coming up on the Greenland icecap. Passengers who'd been dozing immediately perked up and raised their window shades. The weather over the North Atlantic was what passed for clear, but by that time, we were already at FL390.

Of course, everyone was eager to get a glimpse of the magnificent fjords on Greenland's east coast. No such luck. That's more the rule than the exception. I could see practically nothing but white in all directions except straight up.

My preference for the middle road may not seem revolutionary, but it represents a paradigm shift in my attitude from the days when I was confined to Earth. Flying was

We live life forward, but we remember it backwards, and the difference between my memories of that first trip to Telluride in a car and the Mooney hop was a revelation. Too often, it seems we take the vertical element for granted, when in fact, altitude is what allows us to rule the world.

hardly new to me when I made that college trip in 1966, but I didn't own an airplane and had limited money for a rental. My Christmas view of Telluride had been strictly two-dimensional.

Logic dictated that I should have been more inured when I overflew Telluride that first time years ago after a million or so miles had passed beneath my wings. Instead, I was captivated.

We live life forward, but we remember it backwards, and the difference between my memories of that first trip to Telluride in a car and the Mooney hop was a revelation. Too often, it seems, we take the vertical element for granted when, in fact, altitude is what allows us to rule the world.

Wouldn't it be great if you could live in a place such as Telluride? Wouldn't it be terrible if you had to live there without access to an airplane?

24

Ode To The Fast Lane

Can it really be only an incidental century since man discovered the incredibility of powered flight?

I wouldn't want to be riding out on the wing tonight. The wind is roaring down out of the northwest like polar bear's breath, a vicious torrent of air frozen by winter and twisted by the Rocky Mountains. Somewhere below, far down in a blanket of black sky 2-4 miles deep, the night snow of November blitzes New Mexico and Colorado into frozen immobility.

But for me, the night is stars and moon and warm leather and the snore of my engines through the velveteen, obsidian darkness. On the panel before me, two dozen instruments paint impressions of my 200-knot speed, and a half-dozen radios verify that I'm now far from where I was and closer to where I want to be.

Still, I seem to be suspended in my own, private cocoon of immovable comfort, totally detached from the reality of solid ground. The OAT suggests it is minus 30 degrees Celsius outside, but the Janitrol heater is keeping up, and my Zulu headset blocks the noise but lets in the music of Stan Getz, more than a fair trade.

> *The night is stars and moon and warm leather and the snore of my engines through the velveteen, obsidian darkness.*

The engine nacelles on each side glow from the warmth of orange-hot turbochargers, happily spinning at 60,000 rpm, fooling my Continental engines into believing they're breathing the air of Denver instead of compressing the sky at 21,000 feet. I'm alone in the little twin tonight, reaching for Wichita, somewhere out on the plain.

How did we come so far so fast? I wonder behind the gentle chaff of my oxygen mask. Can it really be only an incidental century since man discovered the incredibility of powered flight? Can we really have leaped so high and so far, so fast?

Yes, yes, and yes. It seems somehow a monstrous joke that one of the most significant scientific innovations since the invention of the wheel took nearly 5,500 years to achieve; yet, once realized, progress in the new discipline has been little short of logarithmic.

Until the 19th century, the cleverest form of transportation known to man was the back of a horse, plodding along at perhaps 5 knots. Trains increased that to 40 knots. Today, private air travel is gaining on Mach 1, and 200 knots is becoming boringly commonplace on even single-engine piston aircraft.

Business and professional men and women, doctors, lawyers, bricklayers, plumbers, and homemakers; all are beginning to take airplanes for granted, as both the machines themselves and the pilots who fly them become safer practically every year. The accident record of "those little airplanes" is better than almost any other form of transport; snowmobiling, water skiing, dog sledding, ice boating, off-roading, paragliding, bungee-jumping, and most definitely driving. In 2018, some 36,000 people died on America's highways, while general aviation fatalities amounted to only 387.

In the U.S., there are now something like 600,000 licensed pilots who collectively log 27 million hours a year in 200,000 airplanes. Mobility is becoming a key concept in the business world, and it means more to the recreational traveler, as well. General aviation has proven its worth as an alternative to automobile and airline travel, offering access to thousands more places on your own schedule with all your baggage guaranteed to arrive when you do and no need to take off your shoes before boarding the airplane. Oh, and yes, you *can* bring aboard a bottle of water that you didn't buy at the airport, a life raft, a utility tool, a seeing-eye dog, and a semi-automatic survival shotgun if you wish.

Sadly, pilots still must battle the inanities of the Fourth Estate, and that's not liable to change any time soon. How often have you read something like the following in your local newspaper: "A six-seat, three-engine, Sikorsky Skyhawk crashed today in a vacant field, 60 miles south of Tecumseh, injuring all three pilots on board. Though the light plane went down on a Sunday, 67 miles from the nearest school in July, it could have injured dozens of children had it crashed in a school yard in October. The flight originated from an uncontrolled airport in Krelman, Idaho, suggesting the pilot may have had little control. The weather was perfect at the time, but authorities said no flight plan had been filed, so the pilot obviously had no idea where he was."

In truth, most of us who fly for fun or profit recognize that aviation isn't always art and beauty. Flying can be pure work, irregular hours, fast food, too little sleep, marginal hotels, and plenty of etc. Still, most pilots who make all or part of their income flying anything from Sky-hawks to Boeings wouldn't trade their jobs for anything else.

Whether it's "scuz-bag freighter pilots," as one friend with UPS used to call herself, aviators who fly ambulatory patients on demand, ferry pilots who cross oceans in God-only-knows what kind of airplanes, or airline captains (still regarded as the peak of the pyramid) all acknowledge that flying is a remarkable way to make a living. It's more than coincidence that most pilots who fly for a living have a private aircraft stashed in a hangar back home and often enjoy nothing better than an occasional burger flight on a day off.

I work in this industry full time, so no one needs to convince me of the operational efficiency of general aviation versus the airlines. Even when fuel prices go bananas (or watermelon), pilots are finding that the economics of doing it yourself can make sense.

True, I've had to fly an airline to Oshkosh (though it did seem slightly heretical to travel by airline to worship at the most holy grail of general aviation places), but that was only because I couldn't find anyone to share expenses in my Mooney.

The airlines wouldn't consider operating most flights with a load factor of 25% percent, so why should the math make more sense for a single pilot alone in a four-seat airplane? With two passengers aboard, I could have split the costs three ways and made the trip to OSH in nearly the same door-to-door time at roughly the same cost — and had fun in the process.

As I drift along at an easy 3-plus nautical miles per minute above unseen winter Kansas, outpacing the disembodied lights of cars on the interstate below by a factor of at least three, I can only wonder why every businessman with the means and the need to move people and things from Podunk to Townsville has not discovered the fast lane in the sky.

In truth, most of us who fly for fun or profit recognize that aviation isn't always art and beauty. Flying can be pure work, irregular hours, fast food, too little sleep, marginal hotels, and plenty of etc.

About the Author

Aviation writer/photographer and pilot Bill Cox has been in love with airplanes since the age of 13, though he refuses to admit how long ago that was. He survived his first airplane ride as a Civil Air Patrol Cadet in a Piper J-3 Cub on skis out of Merrill Field in Anchorage, Alaska, sometime in the middle of the last century. "We did a variety of search and rescue missions," Bill commented. "All search and no rescue."

Bill attended the University of Alaska Fairbanks for two years and the University of New Mexico Albuquerque for nearly five years, earning what he now acknowledges were "a pair of marginally useless bachelor's degrees," one in science and one in art (music).

A former aerospace technical writer for Douglas Aircraft, Bill became a full-time, independent, freelance writer in 1974 and has gone on to sell some 2,000 articles. Between 1985 and 1991, Bill worked with then-ABC/TV senior vice president Phil Boyer (now retired AOPA president) as an on-camera host, writer, and primary formation pilot for the ABC/TV series "Wide World of Flying."

Starting in 1977, Bill began delivering new and used aircraft overseas and has made 220 delivery flights across the world. Notably, and not chronicled in this book, Bill delivered Brad Pitt and Angelina Jolie's former Cessna Grand Caravan from Long Beach, California, to its new owner in Seoul, South Korea.

In a half-century of flying, he's had 13 engine failures (including two at one time — see Chapter 11), but has only lost one airplane, a Piper Lance, in the Ogaden Desert of Ethiopia in 1998 (also detailed in Chapter 11).

Bill has logged about 15,000 hours in 60 years of flying. He has set 28 NAA/FAI world speed records and currently holds a commercial certificate with multi-engine, instrument, seaplane, glider, and helicopter ratings.

Bill lives in San Pedro, California, with his better half, Peggy, a veterinarian and also a pilot; his Siberian Husky, Kenai; Australian Cattle Dog, Scout; and flies his sixth airplane, a Lopresti Mooney, though "far too infrequently."

Made in the USA
Monee, IL
10 October 2020